The Larger Parish

and

Group Ministry

THE LARGER PARISH
AND
GROUP MINISTRY

MARVIN T. JUDY

NEW YORK   NASHVILLE

ABINGDON PRESS

SET UP, PRINTED, AND BOUND BY THE
PARTHENON PRESS, AT NASHVILLE,
TENNESSEE, UNITED STATES OF AMERICA

TO

William Edwin Judy

Faithful pastor who died at a
premature age while serving
country churches

Preface

This volume stems from a growing need for a more definitive statement on co-operative plans for administering the work of the church in town and country areas.

It has been my privilege to participate in dozens of meetings during the past ten years in which the work of the rural church was discussed in many sections of the United States, Mexico, and Europe. Inevitably the larger parish, group ministry, and other forms of co-operative plans have been suggested as answers to the problems surrounding the rural church—yet there has been ambiguity as to what such plans are and how they operate.

Different denominations interpret co-operative plans differently. The term "larger parish," for instance, means something vastly different in New England than in the Midwest or South. Yet the philosophy undergirding the original parish movement was sound. Differences of interpretations should not lead to the abandonment of the idea.

This work is attempting to describe the nature of rural culture, the changes taking place in rural society which force the church to make adjustments, and the history and development of the larger parish and group ministry. Also, it attempts to define clearly five types of co-operative programs related to the larger parish and group ministry, and to "spell out" certain tried and tested methods of operation.

In October, 1946, the denominational executives of The Methodist Church in the state of Missouri asked me to leave a happy appointment in St. Louis to become director of the

Harrison County (Missouri) Larger Parish. Seminary had not taught me the meaning of the larger parish, and the term was not too significant. John W. Ward, Sr., district superintendent, saw the need for a co-operative program and stimulated interest in it. Ivan Lee Holt, resident bishop of Missouri, felt that the area to be served was ripe for the harvest. I believe, however, we were all aware of the needs and desirous of ministering to those needs, but we were quite uninformed as to how to go about the work. I became pastor of eight congregations located in small towns and open country, and director of a parish consisting of twenty-seven churches and six ministers (including myself). The name, if I am true to my definitions in Chapter III, was wrong. It was a group ministry, and the charge of eight churches served by myself and a student-assistant was a closely-integrated denominational larger parish.

Floyd V. Brower, an experienced minister in town and country pastorates, was placed on the field by Bishop Holt for three months, and had done a magnificent work in preparing the people in the parish for the new organization and my coming. The district superintendent was always available for help in any phase of the work. He knew how to lend assistance without being obtrusive. Bishop Holt gave more attention to the parish than his time would warrant, visiting the parish four times in five years. E. I. Webber accompanied me to the parish, serving four churches; and upon my leaving in 1952, he became the director. The first staff of the parish consisted of David E. Fields, H. E. Marshall, Elmer Evans, N. R. Eveland, W. W. Miller, E. I. Webber, and myself. Other ministers were added during the five years.

While serving in the parish, I made a systematic study of the literature in the field of the rural church. Counsel was sought with leaders in the rural church, including such persons as the late C. M. McConnell, Rockwell Smith, Aaron Rapking, Dumont Clarke, Herbert E. Stotts, Earl Brewer, James Sells, Glenn F. Sanford, Elliott L. Fisher, A. W. Martin, Ralph L. Woodward, and Lawrence Hepple. Many of these persons visited the parish.

During the last year of my work in the parish, I answered a growing need for a clearer understanding of the sociological forces at play in the rural community by enrolling in Iowa State College of Agriculture and Mechanical Arts at Ames to do graduate studies in rural sociology. The study opened for me a completely new understanding of forces operative in rural culture affecting the town and country church. I am indebted particularly to Ray E. Wakeley, Joseph B. Gittler, Walter A. London, and George Beal for their assistance in helping me to understand more clearly social theory, leadership, rural society, and forces at play in rural culture. The dissertation was a systematic analysis of the Kirksville District in the Missouri Conference of The Methodist Church. Through the excellent cooperation of the district superintendent, Joseph W. Thompson, a detailed analysis of the ten counties of the district was made. On the basis of the study, Dr. Thompson organized several group ministries and larger parishes.

Through continued research, study, contact with rural churches, participation in many types of town and country church conferences, and association with leaders in denominational and interdenominational programs of the rural church, I have come to the following convictions:

1. The principles of the larger parish as envisioned by Harlow S. Mills and his contemporaries in 1911 merit much attention in our present-day attempt to minister to people in rural areas.

2. When proper leadership is available, rural people will re-

9

spond with enthusiastic support of the church with their time, talents, and means.

3. Sound principles of human relationships defined in the studies of sociologists and social psychologists are instruments of immeasurable worth in assisting in church administration.

4. Principles of sound research are essential in approaching the work of the church in town and country areas.

5. The above items, coupled with a dedicated ministry and laity, can mean reformation in rural areas.

This work is written in nontechnical terms. It is aimed at making clear to laymen, ministers, and denominational executives the work of the larger parish and group ministry.

The book was first produced in mimeographed form under the title *Serve to Survive* and used in three teaching experiences during the summer of 1957: Candler School of Theology, Perkins School of Theology, and the Arkansas pastors' school of The Methodist Church. More than one hundred persons have read the book and offered many criticisms. In every case the suggestions have been considered seriously in revision. I am indebted to the students in the schools for their patience in my teaching and frankness of their criticisms. Special thanks goes to the Church and Community Incorporated in Atlanta, Georgia, for asking me to participate in the Church and Community Workshop at Emory University. The leaders, James Sells, Ross Freeman, and Earl Brewer each read the manuscript and made suggestions for changes.

I am indebted also to many others for their help. Decherd H. Turner, Jr., librarian, of Perkins School of Theology carefully criticized chapter by chapter as the first rough manuscript came to life. A. W. Martin, Perkins School of Theology, read and criticized the manuscript. In addition to the above mentioned persons, thanks for reading and making suggestions go to Aaron

10

Rapking, Glenn F. Sanford, Richard Comfort, Sterling Ward, Floyd V. Brower, Floyd R. Curl, and Bishop A. Frank Smith.

Thankful recognition is expressed to Mrs. Lorena Cantrell and Miss Delores Marymee for typing the manuscripts.

And finally a sincere word of thanks to Murlene Judy, who has assisted in keeping me abreast of bibliography in the fields of church and related fields, and above all has been willing to share a vagabond life as wife of a Methodist minister pioneering in the field of town and country church.

MARVIN T. JUDY

Contents

I

THE NATURE
OF RURAL SOCIETY

In the early days of the development of America, pioneer settlers moved across the nation forming a pattern of rural culture peculiar, in most respects, to the United States.[1] The pattern of homesteading was the family-sized farm.

European tradition, from which the pioneer had come, was that of village life with all families living in the village moving out daily to till the soil surrounding the village. Towns in Germany, central Europe, and England, even until this day, are not classified as rural or urban but as industrial or agricultural. If the predominant means of making a living is that of employment in a factory, mill, or mine, the village is industrial. If, on the other hand, the predominant means of livelihood is agriculture, the village is agricultural. The village can be a sizable town or small city even up to as much as 10,000 population.

After the first few years of colonial settlement in America, when it was necessary to build a barricaded shelter for protection from the Indians, the colonists began building their homes on the land they were to cultivate. This pattern was emphasized and encouraged with the opening up of new territory, and "squatter's rights" entitled an individual to become sole owner of the land on which he built his cabin. The Homestead Act of 1862 increased the emphasis upon land ownership and living upon the land one tilled, making it possible for an operator of a farm to become owner if he lived on the land for a stated time. "Possession is nine points of the law" became a slogan meaning if one was on the land, he had a nine-to-one chance of becoming owner of it.

As families settled on the land in the open country, there was a usual pattern of institutional development: first, they built their cabins; second, they built a school; third, they built a church. Someone with an enterprising ambition built a store which became a general merchandising institution selling anything from a spool of thread to a full set of harness.

The school, church, and store served an area geographically small—usually, as far as the church and school were concerned, not more than three to five miles radius. The people living in this service area of the church and school were dependent upon each other in several ways: fellowship and social life, mutual aid in times of disaster and sickness, mutual assistance in busy farming seasons. Thus there grew up a neighborhood symbolized in a name: Big Sandy, Bald Knob, Liberty, Bethel, Mt. Moriah, and a thousand other names.

THE RURAL NEIGHBORHOOD DEFINED

Thus, the rural neighborhood was born. In the pioneer days of settlement of the nation, the neighborhood played a vital

16

role. It was the center of elementary school activities. In it was the church—one or more congregations. In the neighborhood were to be found a general merchandise store, a blacksmith shop, and sometimes a medical doctor. The neighborhood was isolated due to poor roads and slow transportation. It was necessary for a church and school to be established within the neighborhood structure if the people of the area were to have educational and religious opportunities. A neighborhood was compelled to be self-sufficient in most respects. Only the merchant made his way, with any degree of regularity, out of the neighborhood for the purpose of replenishing his supply of goods.

In the intimacy of the neighborhood, children were born, reared, educated, nurtured in religious living, married, found their place in the economy of the area, and conformed to the mores of the group. The cemetery became a part of the neighborhood structure usually close to the one-room church.

Such neighborhoods, three to five miles in diameter, have become the romantic symbol of rural America. It has been the little red schoolhouse where many of our American statesmen and leaders have found their early training. Stories and novels have been written by the score about romantic pioneer America.

The rural neighborhood has been the subject of many studies by rural sociologists. Entire texts have been devoted to the study of rural society with primary emphasis upon the rural neighborhood. Among the many definitions the most common is: "A rural neighborhood consists of an area in which people neighbor together; that is, visit, borrow tools and equipment, trade work, and cooperate in various other ways."[2] The rural neighborhood is usually composed of ten to twenty families living closely enough to visit one another, developing a common bond of friendship. There may be one or more institutions in the rural neighborhood. This can be a church, elementary school,

17

general store, or a combination of these. There may be no institutions, but merely a social unit built around fellowship of common interests.

The rural neighborhood is rapidly changing. Good roads, modern automobiles and trucks, have made the agricultural town, or even the distant city, very close to the residents of the neighborhood. The general merchandise store has dwindled in business until no longer does it have an adequate trade to warrant operation. Thousands of such crossroads stores have ceased to be. It takes less time for the rural neighborhood family to drive five to fifteen miles to town than it did for their grandparents to go three miles for their trading.

The one-room country school all across America is rapidly becoming a memory. Good roads and the school bus have brought consolidation forcing the children to go to the larger school in town or a new consolidated school in a different neighborhood. Through state control of funds, consolidation has been forced upon many rural neighborhoods whether the people wanted it or not. General opinion, however, is that consolidation is worth what it cost in neighborhood morale by the compensation of a much better quality of education than is possible in the one-room, one-teacher school.

Neighborhood rural churches by the thousands have suffered a like fate to that of the stores and schools. It has been estimated that the Protestant Church of America has been closing one thousand rural churches a year since 1930. There is no question but many of these churches have served their period of usefulness. They have been the source of Christian guidance through the decades. The primary difficulty has been that there has been no systematic procedure devised by denominational executives for the closing of a rural church. The usual pattern has been that the church continued to weaken until the few remaining

18

members became so discouraged they finally, with a sigh, just let the program of the church go.

Sometimes the closing of a rural church has led to the reviving of a village church. The leaders in the rural church simply move their membership to a town or village church. However, the larger group of people in the rural church have not aligned themselves with another church, and are lost to the membership of the church and left without a church home. This pattern calls for some systematic method of neighborhood study to be made before a church closes or is consolidated with another church.

In spite of the thousands of rural neighborhood churches which have closed in recent years, there are still thousands of them in existence. In The Methodist Church alone, there are approximately 15,000 rural neighborhood churches. Lawrence Hepple, reporting to the National Convocation on the Church in Town and Country, October, 1956, on some findings from his four-year study of the rural church in Missouri, states:

Open country churches [rural neighborhood churches] were located an average of 3.8 miles from another open country church, and an average of 6.7 miles from a church of the same denomination. At the time of the survey there was approximately one open country church for every 16 square miles in rural Missouri. In other words, on the average there was a rural church within two miles from every farm family. These numerous small and part-time religious groups may be maintained for a period of time, but it is well for the church administrators to re-examine the number and location of rural churches in relation to the total program of their respective religious bodies.[3]

What is the future of the rural neighborhood? This is a question the rural sociologist is asking across America. In the early thirties the opinion prevailed that the rural neighborhood was rapidly ceasing to be. Such an attitude aided in public-school consolidation. But, in a few years the sociologist was saying that the rural neighborhood was persisting—it was going to remain, at least for a time, as a part of American culture. It was discovered that when the school went out of existence, when the church had died, when the store was gone, informal groups sprang up. They were primarily for the purpose of fellowship, and the desire of the individual for communication with friends of like mind. In more recent years there has been a re-emphasis upon the vanishing rural neighborhood. Sociologists are not agreed. It is possible that the rural neighborhood is ceasing to function as an organizational unit, but will remain as a social unit. Some sociologists believe that it is a part of the rural culture the same as the family, and plays a vital role in cultural development.

In the midst of such change stands the rural church. In spite of the thousands of churches that have been closed, there are still tens of thousands of them. In some areas of America today, seventy per cent of the Protestant congregations are in open country. Most of these churches are small. Many of the churches must share a minister with another congregation. Many do not know the value of a well-rounded program of church activity.

What will be the fate of the neighborhood church? The answer to this question depends upon the strategy of the Protestant church in town and country areas. Two general hypotheses can now be stated for serving people by the church in rural areas: (1) If the neighborhood church is needed as a unifying force in the rural neighborhood, the Christian community is duty-bound to keep it there and provide an opportunity for a full program of church activity. (2) If the church is not needed as an institution within the neighborhood for a unifying force, then the people who reside there must be provided ministerial leadership and a church in which they may express their religious devotion. This church will be in another neighborhood or community center. If in the latter case, some means of drawing the people of the neighborhood together with people of the area in which the church is located, must be discovered. It is possible that through a common trade center, consolidated schools, farm organizations, and church activities, the people will have built natural affinities with one another. The major tragedy of the declining and dying neighborhood church has been that large groups of people have been left without a church tie of any kind. Neighborhood ties are so strong that there is no feeling of oneness with people of another neighborhood; yea, frequently feelings of animosity are felt between neighborhood groups preventing the affiliation with a church in another neighborhood.[4]

THE RURAL COMMUNITY

The second cultural area in rural society is the rural community. The word "community" is being widely used by theologian, philosopher, and sociologist. The word is derived from the Latin *communis*, meaning fellowship, or community of relations of feeling. In Medieval Latin it was used in the sense of a body of fellows or fellow townsmen. MacIver, in an early attempt at defining community, said, "By community I mean any area of common life, village, or town, or district, or country, or even wider area. To deserve the name community, the area must be somehow distinguished from further area, the common life may have some characteristics of its own such that the frontiers of the area have some meaning." [5] Kenyon L. Butterfield in 1918 distinguished the community from the neighborhood:

I wish to emphasize one point strongly. We must not confuse "community" with "neighborhood." A neighborhood is simply a group of families living conveniently near together. The neighborhood can do a great many things, but it is not a community. A true community is a social group that is more or less self-sufficient. It is big enough to have its own center of interest—its trading center, its social center, its own church, its own school house, its own garage, its own library, and to possess such other institutions as the people of the community need. It is something more than a mere aggregation of families. There may be several neighborhoods in a community. A community is the smallest social unit that will hold together. . . . A community is a sort of individualized group of people. It is both the smallest and the largest number of people that can constitute a real social unit. It is a sort of family of families.[6]

Butterfield would have his reader recognize a distinct difference between neighborhood and community. *This is important in our study for an understanding of the problems related to the rural church.* Sociologists have come to think of the rural community as consisting of a central town or village surrounded by several rural neighborhoods. In the central town will be found a sufficient number of institutions, as Butterfield so ably states above, to supply the day-by-day needs of the villager and the residents of the rural neighborhoods. Dwight Sanderson in 1920 stated: "A rural community consists of the people in a local area tributary to the center of their common interests. The community is the smallest geographical unit of organized association of the chief human activities." [7] This definition has been the basis of many research projects, and, along with the methods of community delineation, has come what is probably the most universally accepted definition of rural community: "A rural community consists of the social interaction of people and their institutions in the local area in which they live on dispersed farm-steads and in a hamlet or village which forms the center of their common interests." [8] With Sanderson's insights as the basis of community definition, a working statement of the meaning of community is presented for the sake of analysis:

1. People and/or institutions in social interaction
2. A definable geographical area
3. A psychic feeling among individuals which gives a feeling of "identity-with"
4. An understood relationship which controls the mores of the community life
5. A constellation of institutions and services rendered for the benefit of the people of the community

A brief discussion of each of the above is presented.

1. *People and/or institutions in social interaction.* Within the community structure there must be mutual sharing of time, energy, social activities, and institutional life. Every rural community has in it the opportunity for people to come in contact with one another. Families mix together in church, school, and business organizations and are constantly having interaction either in co-operation or conflict. But at any rate, people are thrown together in common everyday activities. Individuals are known in their relations that naturally evolve out of such associations.

2. *A certain definable geographical area.* The territory for intimate social interaction is naturally limited by geography. There is a limit to which people can travel for trade, institutional, and social life. A later chapter will deal with methods of determining the geographical community boundary. This is a vitally important factor in church administrative areas.

3. *A psychic feeling among individuals which gives a feeling of "identity with."* The residents of a community quickly come

23

to identify themselves with the community in which they reside. One can ask the question, "What is your community?" and an answer will be given, "Pleasant Valley" or "Centerville." There is a loyalty developed in the mind of the resident. This is expressed in civic pride, support of school athletic groups, church, and community enterprises.

4. *An understood relationship which controls the mores of the community life.* Every community has personality. Customs are established which carry over from generation to generation. Many times customs are difficult to change and become detriments to progress. Moral standards are established. Individuals who break out of such standards receive the condemnation of the group. One can observe the customs, beliefs, and attitudes of a rural community, and type it in a single sentence.

5. *A constellation of institutions and services rendered for the benefit of the people of the community.* All people are in need of certain services to maintain normal existence. For instance, everyone must have a basic way of making a living, a means of educating their children, a means of worship and religious expression, social contacts and recreation, communication with others through voice and written page, a doctor, and a lawyer. Therefore, there are six services which the community will supply in part or all together: (1) economic, (2) educational, (3) religious, (4) social, (5) communicative, and (6) professional. Most of these needs are supplied through organized services rendered to people.

A brief analysis of each service is presented: (1) A community must offer its residents resources to make a living. There must be adequate job opportunities, a soil strong enough to support its owner or renter, or businesses or industries in which one can sell one's services. Without adequate economic resources, community structure soon disintegrates. (2) All people stand in need of education. Formalized education has been provided for in the development of an intricate program of public education. Community life consists of opportunities to educate children, youth, and adults. Through special programs of adult education, the chance for a continual development of the intellect should be provided. (3) Religious needs have been a part of every civilization since the beginning of the history of man. The community must provide through its institutions opportunities for worship and the expression of one's religious faith. (4) Social relationships are as deeply rooted in the human structure as religious desires. All people have the herd instinct. They want to associate with friends. They want to do things together during leisure hours. The community structure must consider this fact and provide opportunities for such association. Commercialized social and recreational activities have become a part of the American culture. The movie house, the park, swimming pool, and less desirable forms of commercialized recreation are a part of the community structure. (5) All communities must provide resources for communications of its people within the group. Transportation facilities must be adequate. Road systems in our modern culture are proving to be a decided pattern of rural community development. The telephone communication is an important function of community structure. With the breakdown of the rural telephone system since 1920 and the refusal of public utility companies to rebuild rural lines, the rural electrification co-operatives are moving into the area of building a strong communication system among rural people. The town weekly newspaper has been a source of important rural community communication. (6) Professional services must be available for all people. There are legal matters which require the services of a lawyer, physical needs requiring the services of a doctor, religious needs requiring services of a minister. In the

25

community structure, these needs must be provided for. One of the difficulties facing the small rural community is the fact that professional people have refused to live among and serve rural people. This phenomenon is one of the deciding factors in the development of the enlarged community structure described below.

With the above definition of a rural community and the six types of services rendered by the community before the reader, it will be seen immediately that it is not possible for each rural community to have all of these services available. Therefore, to a certain extent, the number of services in a community determines the size of the community. Communities, then, are classified in various categories. According to Kolb and Brunner, there are five types of communities, dependent upon the extent of the services provided to the constituent members of the community:[9] (1) Single service community. It is composed of people living in a village and open country with only one of the six services available. This is an elementary school, a church, a general store. Seldom does such a community consist of more than two hundred people in the village center. (2) Limited service type community. More than one service, but not all six, are offered and made available in the community structure. It is a territory around and a village of two hundred to five hundred inhabitants. Approximately eighty per cent of the trade of such a community center is drawn from the area around the central village. (3) Semi-complete service type community. The central village or town of five hundred to one thousand inhabitants offers most of the six major services, but not necessarily all. Approximately seventy-five per cent of the trade in the central town is drawn from the surrounding area. (4) The complete, partially specialized service type community. The central town is composed of one thousand to five thousand inhabitants.

It offers to its residents all six services and may offer some specialized services, such as a small hospital. It may be the county-seat town with several lawyers. There may be small factories, advanced opportunities for learning, recreational facilities, and so forth. Approximately fifty per cent of the trade of the town is drawn from the surrounding community rural area. (5) The urban or highly specialized service community. All six services are offered in the community center, plus fields of specialization in all areas.

The services rendered in the community center become the means of drawing the boundary lines of the community outreach. This is discussed more fully in Chapter VII. It is sufficient to state that the rural community is composed of a geographic area with one village or town surrounded by several rural neighborhoods. The central town is the center of common activities and from which the people of the area derive, for the most part, their primary or day-by-day services.

In the structure of modern rural life, the community is vitally important as a social unit. The development of a strategy for the church in the community setting, considering natural affinities, is one of the tasks of the church. It is possible, for instance, to develop a program within a community structure that could not be developed between two communities. To attempt a program of closely integrated work in two communities is to invite defeat. Churches attached together for a circuit, yoke-field, or parish, should be in the same community for harmony. There is frequently a high degree of jealousy and competition between contiguous rural communities. Athletic contests, the competition for business, competition for receiving county or state aid for maintaining public schools or roads—all lead to friction between communities. Such friction inevitably creeps into the church and can spell defeat in co-operative programs. A *clear*

27

comprehension of the neighborhood and community concept is one of the first essentials for the development of a strong program of the church in town and country areas.

THE ENLARGED COMMUNITY

The third sociological unit in rural society is the enlarged community. To date, there has been little scientific research on the enlarged community comparable to that for the rural neighborhood and community. This is, no doubt, because it is a rather recent development and has come with the consolidation of schools and good highways. An enlarged community consists of two or more rural communities bound together in a natural or political area, with a dominant town in which all communities have a common interest. This is frequently synonymous with a county or part of a county. Figure I maps the typical rural neighborhood, rural community, and enlarged community.

There are many things which draw rural people together within the county structure. All people have the same county government. Services of the county agricultural agencies are at the command of all people in the county. School supervision, even to a county school board, is established on a wider perspective than the local community. Consolidation of high schools has brought the mind of the people to think beyond their local area. There are some sociologists who now feel the rural county—that is, a county with the central town no larger than 2,500 people—is becoming more "community-like." In other words, the qualities of community as described above are applicable to the entire county. Approximately one half of the counties in the United States, or 1,500, fall in this classification.

There are hundreds of counties in the nation which have towns of more than 2,500 population which are still rural in their outlook. Many counties have towns of five thousand, ten

28

thousand, or even as large as twenty thousand which are dependent primarily upon the agricultural operations in the surrounding area for their major economic activities. These counties, though not rural in the technical sense as defined by the United States Census, are rural in their outlook. Enlarged communities are formed around such towns and become important administrative units for the church.

For all practical purposes in rural church administration, the county serves as the basis of study. Population data, information on housing, agriculture, business, and industry can be secured on the county basis. There are areas of co-operation in church work by all churches in the county which cannot be accomplished by churches in adjoining counties. One must always be mindful of the rural community structure within a county, however, and recognize there are limitations to what can be done beyond the rural community. In subsequent chapters, organizational procedures within the enlarged community area will be discussed. With approximately one half of the counties in the United States classified as rural, one can readily see how important this unit is in the structure of rural America.

Natural barriers, such as rivers, lakes, mountains, and forests, may divide a county into two or more enlarged community groups. Another factor may be the existence of two towns of near the same size. If there is, for instance, a town of two thousand population which is the county seat, and a town of 2,500 which is not the county seat, there most likely will be much friction between them. This may make it impossible for the two towns to work together.

Other counties may have a larger town, up to ten thousand population, and a subordinate town of 2,500. It is possible that an enlarged community would be around each of these towns or one of them, not including the other. Therefore, it may be said

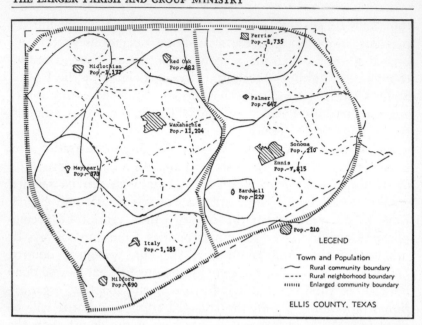

Source: *Methodism in Ellis County, Texas, 1955.* By Marvin T. Judy.

FIGURE I. Ellis County, Texas. The three meaningful sociological units, rural neighborhood, rural community, and enlarged community, are illustrated in the above map of Ellis County, Texas. Major delineation was done on the basis of traffic-flow map.

that the enlarged community consists of one dominant town with one or more subdominant towns and their surrounding rural neighborhoods, bound together by natural, political, or trade affinities.

As the larger parish and group ministry are defined in subsequent pages, it will be seen how important the natural sociological grouping in rural culture is to good administrative procedures. It can be stated at this point, though the reader will

30

understand more fully as he proceeds through the book: *the closely integrated larger parish, either denominational or inter-denominational, will function for maximum efficiency within only one rural community; the loosely integrated larger parish or group ministry can function within either one rural community or an enlarged community.*

II

TRENDS IN RURAL AMERICA
AFFECTING THE TOWN
AND COUNTRY CHURCH

In the society in which we find ourselves, we are aware that we are the recipients of all that has gone into the past developing that which is commonly known as our culture. We are the products of it, and at the same time the creators of an ever-changing new culture to emerge in a new society which shall follow us. We live in a society which is not static but dynamic. A dynamic society is one which is changing. Some changes as far as the moral and cultural good of mankind is concerned are good; some are bad. Only the future can tell the final outcome of the effects of our living of the day. Changes are inevitable in a growing society. Changes always bring a tension between the new and the old. Changes call for a rethinking of the old, a re-evaluating of the old, a preservation through concerted effort of values in old things. New things must stand upon their own merit. They must establish themselves in the minds of people for their worth. Sometimes old and new must be brought into a synthesis for the preservation of an old value in a new idea.

A part of the thrill of living comes through the processes of change. New challenges, opportunities, the expansion of one's intellectual pursuits, all lead to a thrilling experience of life itself. This could have been in the mind of Jesus as he said, "I am not come to destroy, but to fulfill." Fulfillment in this sense means to complete, to continue, to build upon. Modern society must take that which has been handed to it through the accumulative culture and tradition, and build upon it toward a more constructive way of life. Life can be abundant when a full comprehension of the expansion of God's kingdom is realized, and when it is realized that his kingdom is an ever-growing, expanding culture for all the age—every age of mankind.

Change and transition in society happen. This is to say, change is not a planned something, the end result of which is predictable and exact. Change takes place usually without a serious consciousness of the change taking place by those of the social order. Individuals and groups become aware that "things are not as they used to be." Some bemoan this fact. Some become discouraged and cease trying to do much about the old order. Some rationally look the change squarely in the face and adjust a program and life to meet it. Thus we are always confronted with the necessity of facing frankly what is happening to our society, what is happening to our fellow beings, what is happening to us, and what are the factors that have contributed to these changes.

Anyone whose life spans two, or a part of two, generations in contact with rural America must be aware that many changes have taken place in rural life. These changes have affected home

33

life, community life, church life, and school life. Most of the changes have come gradually, without the masses of the populace being aware of how much the changes have affected the total of life. It has resulted in a state of frustration on the part of church, school, and community leaders in many areas. A sense of futility has gripped the mind of many a leader. Others have accepted the challenge of change and are ready to do something about meeting new demands as they arise.

With this brief background, a survey of the changes which have taken place in rural culture within recent years is presented. A word of definition is necessary before we go further. What is meant by the words "rural" and "urban" and the term "town and country"?

Rural, in its simplest definition, applies to all territory where there are fewer than 2,500 people living in a cluster of population known as a town or village. Urban is any area in which there are as many as 2,500 people living in an incorporated or unincorporated place. The 1950 definition of rural and urban included "metropolitan area," which includes the concentration of population, usually an entire county, in which there is a city of fifty thousand persons or more. Thus many persons are included in the urban population in 1950 who had not been before that date. The term "town and country" as used in many church circles applies to all territory including communities of ten thousand population or less. Some denominations set the figure at five thousand. This expansion of the idea of rurality is due to the fact that sound church administrative policies are so closely related in the churches in towns of ten thousand and less, and open country. This will be amply illustrated in succeeding pages.

Rural, however, goes far deeper than simply an arbitrary population dividing line. There is not space here to elaborate the point, but it must be borne in mind that fundamental characteristics of rural life are quite definable in contrast to urbanity.

Rural and urban societies in their complex differences have been a subject of study by sociologists in both Europe and America for almost a century. Literature describing these polar types, rurality and urbanity, is abundant. It is not the purpose of this writing to go into detail on these differences, but since the basic assumption of this work is concerned with the preservation of the church in town and country areas, and one of the problems of the church is the blending of rural and urban cultures, a brief review is given as a summary of rural and urban traits.[1]

Rural farm people make their living from agricultural pursuits and are concerned with the producing of raw materials from the soil. Residents in the agricultural town, though not producing from the soil, are so closely related to farm population that weather, seasons, crops, agricultural life, are all areas of vital concern. Urban people are interested in the producing of finished products through manufacturing and processing of raw materials. They work by the clock, not by the natural seasons of the year. They are interested in weather, but only as it affects their physical action, fuel bill, air conditioning, and week-end excursions into the country. Rural people are close to nature and are constantly reminded of the Creator as his world moves through the seasons with unremitting regularity. The urban dweller sees man-made things—buildings, mortar, cement.

The basic unit of rural culture is the family. It works together in the making of a living, sharing a common enterprise. The neighborhood, composed of a group of families, is a place of sharing mutual needs in times of catastrophe and times of festive enjoyment. Weddings, family dinners, school gatherings, church functions, all bring the families of a neighborhood together.

35

Such associations make for the development of security and personality. The city is not built around the family. Individuality is stressed as the members of the family go their separate ways for work, education, recreation—and often for church.

With the concentration of population in urban areas there are more incidents of communicable disease, suicide, mental breakdown, and crime than is found in rural areas. The moral state of a predominantly urban culture has been quite sad throughout the history of civilization.

Rural dwellers are traditionally conservative. They reverence tradition, custom, and "old things." On the contrary, urban dwellers are concerned with new things, breaking of tradition, exploration. When either of these traits predominates, a society is in danger. Pure conservatism hampers experimentation, exploration, and progress. Pure liberalism, on the other hand, will lose the "experience of the ages" which has made for depth of living, an appreciation of human values, and a respect for individuality. All that has gone into the development of a traditional culture is not bad. Tried and tested methods of human associations can lead to the discovery of basic ideals to regulate life. To divorce a people from their culture when many traits in that culture have been basically sound in the development of normal, harmonious, and happy living, can spell disaster.

Both segments of society, rural and urban, are needed to maintain a healthy balance. Rural areas need the city to develop a technology for modern agricultural methods. No longer is it necessary for the ruralite to make his living by "the bending of the back." No longer does the rural dweller have to be deprived of modern conveniences in the home which take away the drudgery of living. Rural life needs the city to absorb its surplus of population, for the rural areas of America are still producing far more children than they can gainfully employ back into their

36

economy. The rural areas need the city to purchase the raw materials for food, fiber, and building.

On the other hand, the city needs the rural area to supply it with the basic materials for manufacturing, for man power, for the food to fill the shelves and refrigerators of its massive supermarkets. Urban areas need the conservative, inherently religious nature of the rural culture to maintain individuality, religiousness, integrity, and morality in the midst of anonymous living. Urban areas need the beauty of nature—field, stream, lake, mountain, and forest—as a playground where their dwellers can find release from tension and drudgery of city living.

With travel by highway, rail, and air, and communications by radio, television, and the daily press, there is a constant blending of the above rural-urban traits. A healthy society needs to retain many of the characteristics usually found in rural culture. A nation should strive to preserve "rurality" if for no other reason than to save itself from physical decay. Now to discuss some of the trends in rural life.

DEMOGRAPHIC OR POPULATION CHANGES— RURAL-URBAN SHIFTS

Using the dividing line between rural and urban as 2,500, it is seen that in one hundred years the United States has changed from 86 per cent rural and 14 per cent urban to 37 per cent rural and 63 per cent urban. The decade 1940 to 1950 was a time of exceedingly fast growth of cities, resulting from a great migration of people from rural areas to cities. In every census period except one since 1920, as many as one thousand counties in the nation have lost population, while the national increase has been rising steadily every year. It is a safe hypothesis that most townships or census precincts which do not have in them a major town have lost population in the past thirty years.

Between 1940 and 1950, 1,510 of our 3,070 counties in the nation showed a decline in population. The great gain in population of the nation in the past decade was in urban areas. Four fifths of the population gain between 1940 and 1950 took place in the 168 standard metropolitan areas of the nation. The loss in population in the 1,510 counties in the United States in the ten-year period was, by and large, in the areas outside of towns of less than 2,500 people. Hundreds of small towns lost population. Thousands of rural communities found the population had depleted greatly when the 1950 census was completed. Figure II graphs changes in farm population with a projection to 1975. This fact has led many church administrators to say that the attention of the church must be focused upon the city, for the rural areas are losing all the people. It goes without saying that the great increase in population in urban areas demands a keen church strategy and tremendous extension programs, but it also means a review of the work of the church in rural areas must be made and sound administrative policies forthcoming. There are still 61,796,897 people in rural America as reported in the 1950 census. The church must not forsake the sacred trust of administering the Word of God to this vast multitude.

CHANGES IN RURAL FARM
AND RURAL NONFARM POPULATION

Rural life in the United States has always carried with it the connotation of agricultural living. When tabulations of the 1950 census were complete, the rural farm population contained 24,500,000 persons, or less than one half of the total rural population. This is the first time in the history of the United States that this situation has prevailed. This means that in a nation which had its beginning as an agricultural society, there was in 1956 only 13.3 per cent of the population on farms. Figure III

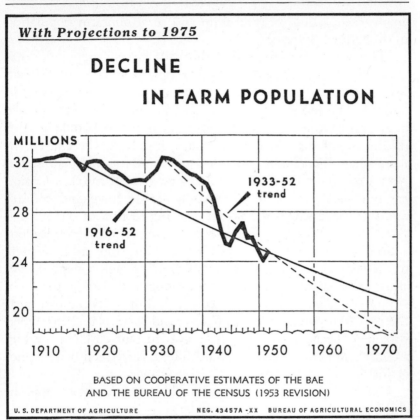

With Projections to 1975

DECLINE
IN FARM POPULATION

BASED ON COOPERATIVE ESTIMATES OF THE BAE
AND THE BUREAU OF THE CENSUS (1953 REVISION)

U. S. DEPARTMENT OF AGRICULTURE   NEG. 43457A-XX   BUREAU OF AGRICULTURAL ECONOMICS

FIGURE II. The only period of significant increase in farm population in the United States during this century was in 1932, and resulted from the economic depression. There has been a consistent and rapid decline since 1932, and all predictions based on past performance indicate the decrease will continue. As long as economic opportunities are in urban areas, and there is a decline in opportunities for gainful employment in farm regions, it is safe to say that the rural farm population will continue to decrease.

39

graphs comparisons of rural farm and rural nonfarm population in the United States.

There are several effects that this shift in rural population has upon the church. First: rural farm people have been traditionally conservative. Rural nonfarm people are usually more liberal in outlook. This brings a decided conflict in the minds of the people in a rural community. Sometimes rural nonfarm people are not readily accepted in rural-farm groups, especially the church. In some areas the rapidly growing rural nonfarm population has put a strain upon the church building facilities. Church extension has not kept pace with this section of the town and country ministry, since this is the fastest growing section of our population. It calls for careful planning upon the part of church leaders.

Second: there is a tendency for migration from urban centers to the fringe areas around the cities as city dwellers desire to get away from crowded housing conditions and into a rural environment. This is developing the commuter community near the city. Many rural churches have found themselves surrounded with new dwellers who have from two to four children needing a church and church-school home. There is frequently a conflict of ideologies which must be faced and overcome.

Third: the rural population is disproportionately large in children and elderly people and lacking in young people and young adults. Rural parents have more children to support than do their city friends. The ratio of adults to those twenty years of age and younger is quite revealing of this fact. In urban areas there are 172 adults for each 100 children and young people under twenty years of age. In the rural-farm population there are 77.6 adults to each 100 children and young people under twenty years of age. As young people mature and become independent of their parents, they must seek gainful employment. Failing to find such employment in their own communities, they are compelled

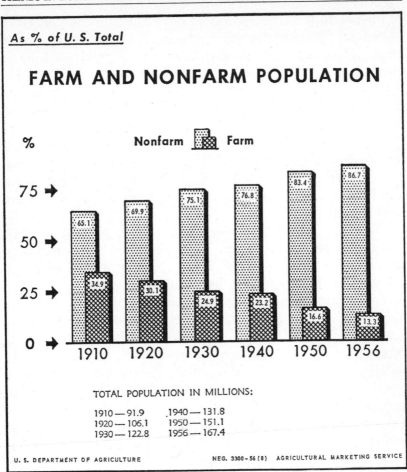

FIGURE III. In 1950, for the first time in the history of the United States, the rural nonfarm population exceeded the rural farm population. In 1950 the rural nonfarm population contained 20.6 per cent of the total, and rural farm population contained 15.6 per cent. By 1956 the farm population in the United States was 13.3 per cent of the total population.

to migrate to the larger town and city. This is a constant drain upon rural financial resources. Consider, for instance, the cost of rearing, feeding, clothing, and educating a child until he is twenty years of age. This is a cash outlay by the rural dweller. After the expenditure of funds the child then migrates to the city. There he becomes a part of our great industrial order, selling his time and services to industry.[2] It has been roughly estimated that in the decade from 1940 to 1950, enough young people migrated from rural areas to the city areas to represent an investment of about two billion dollars. This may account for a part of the problem which so often surrounds the support of the rural church.

The rural areas of the United States are still the seedbed of the surplus population. A simple way to reflect birth rates is to secure the fertility ratio. This is the number of children under five years of age for each one thousand women between the ages of fifteen and forty-four years. In 1950, the fertility ratio was 525 in the rural farm population, 523 in rural nonfarm population, and 383 in the urban population in the United States. It takes a fertility ratio of approximately 370 to maintain the stability of the population of births over deaths. Thus it is readily seen that the rural areas of the nation are producing the surplus of children while the cities are barely holding their own. Yet, the cities are growing with great speed and rural areas continue to lose population. There is only one answer—migration from rural to urban areas. Figure IV illustrates the relative size of families in different segments of the population. This is an extremely important factor in church administration. It has been estimated that ninety per cent of the people uniting with the church on profession of faith or confirmation, do so by the time they are eighteen years of age. Can it be that one of the reasons we have so many unchurched young people in our nation is due

42

to the inadequate program of the church in rural areas? Urban churches are dependent upon rural-urban migration for their growth. The urban birth rate will simply replace the deaths in the church. If the masses of young people migrating to the cities from rural areas are not reached for the church before they leave home, it is a fact that few of them will be reached in later life. The trend in birth rates is toward a more equal rate within urban and rural populations; however, it remains to be seen how long, if ever, the urban birth rate will be as large as the rural.

OFF-FARM WORK BY FARMERS

Another factor affecting the program of the church in rural areas is the large number of days spent by farmers in off-farm work. Many farmers find it necessary to supplement their income by doing work of various kinds in business or industry off the farm. There has been a steady rise in this type of work since 1934. Quoting from Arthur Raper, social scientist in the Bureau of Agricultural Economics:

Along with the decline in the number of farms, the proportion of farm operators who supplement their incomes by working off the farm has increased. The proportion of farm operators doing 100 days or more of off-farm work during the year increased from 11.5 per cent in 1929 to 23.5 per cent in 1949. The number of farm operators reporting 100-249 days of off-farm work remained fairly constant from 1929 to 1939; between 7 and 9 per cent. In the next five years there was a slight decrease. Data for 1949 are not available. Farm operators who worked 250 days or more off-farm work during the year registered the greatest gain, increasing from 4 per cent in 1929 to 12 per cent in 1944. Thus the slight decline in the 100-249 days group was much more than compensated for by the sharp rise in the group doing 250 days or more off-farm work. Between 1939 and 1944, the proportion of all farm operators reporting 250 days or

43

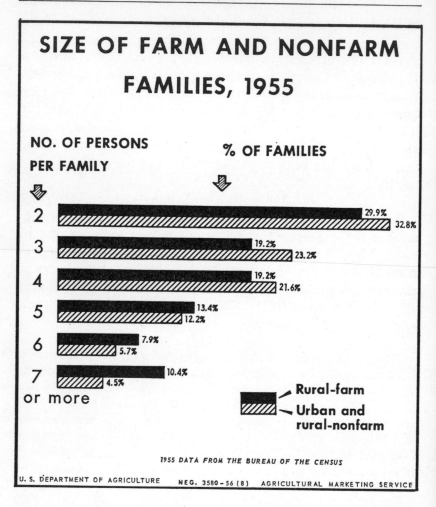

FIGURE IV. About 13.3 per cent of the people of the country are now living on farms. This is a great change since 1910 when 35 per cent lived on farms. Farm families average somewhat larger than nonfarm families.

more practically doubled. When holidays, sickness, and vacations are allowed for, 250 days of off-farm employment is virtually full-time off-farm employment.[3]

A report in Ohio reveals there are more farmers who are members of labor unions than of farm organizations.

With almost one fourth of the farm operators spending one hundred days or more in gainful employment off the farm each year, there are some noticeable effects that this has upon the rural church. It means that there is a divided outlook in the life of the farmer. He is usually a part of two communities. It means he has less time for the work of his church, for social activities, and for family life within his home neighborhood. It often means shift work taking the farmer out of the neighborhood at night and seven days a week. It means an added burden to the family to tend to the usual chores of feeding stock, milking, and tending to crops. It means a continual blending of the rural and urban mentalities. It is safe to say that as long as there is a demand for labor in industry there will continue to be an increase in the number of farm operators spending more time in off-farm employment. Figure V is a graphic description of the situation.

SOME REASONS FOR DEMOGRAPHIC CHANGES

(1) *Farm output and labor input.* The mechanization of agriculture with the coming of the tractor and machines of all types to lighten the farm labor load has made it possible for fewer men to do more work.

Farm output per man-hour is more than twice what it was 40 years ago. The greater part of this increase has taken place in recent years —in fact, 71 per cent in the last 15 years. The number of man-hours worked on farms—excepting only the preliminary estimate for 1951— has been a general decrease for the last quarter-century, and the total output has increased greatly. Taking the period 1935-39 as the baseline, the number of hours of farm-labor input in this country had dropped about 11 per cent by 1951. During the same period total farm production rose nearly 46 per cent. It is significant that a marked increase in farm production has been achieved in the last few years with a decrease in the amount of human effort required.[4]

With the use of machinery and the increasing of the man-hour output, there is less need for farm labor than there was a number of years ago (See Figures VI and VII). Also, a farmer can handle far more land than he once did and must expand his operations in order to support his increasing cost of production. The average size of the American farm has increased in the period 1900 to 1950 from 146 acres to 215 acres. In some areas of the nation one farm has engulfed from one to five farms, supplanting that many families. It is easy to see that this trend makes migration an absolute necessity for those who are forced to seek employment in other ways.

(2) *Depletion of the soil.* An adequate level of living in rural areas is dependent upon adequate soil. When fertility of the soil is depleted, it soon follows that community life is depleted. It is a well-known fact among rural people that the citizens of the United States have been plunderers of the natural resources of our nation. It is estimated that fifty million acres of once fertile cropland have been destroyed or abandoned as productive land. Another hundred million acres have lost from 25 to 75 per cent of productivity through misuse and erosion. Thousands of people still live on this land but do not depend upon it for a living. This is one reason for so many days worked off the farm in gainful employment. It is a safe hypothesis that wherever land is depleted in its fertility, the level of living is low, school facilities are poor, and the church is having a struggle for ex-

46

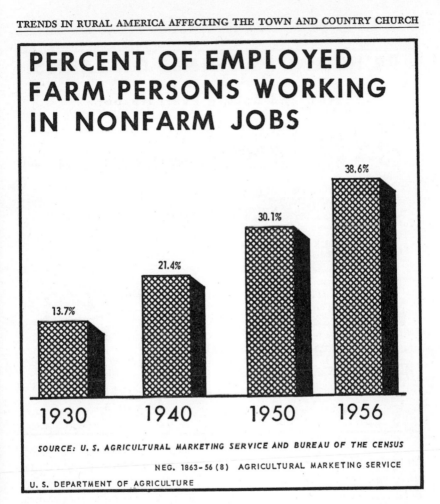

FIGURE V. Farm families are becoming increasingly dependent on income from work off their farms. The proportion of employed farm persons working at nonfarm jobs increased 30 per cent to nearly 40 per cent between 1950 and 1956. The latest Census of Agriculture, that for 1954, shows that 28 per cent of the farm operators worked over 100 days off their farms.

47

FIGURE VI. Since January 1, 1940, the demand for farm products has increased, farm wages have risen, and number of farm workers has declined. These changes have helped to speed up farm mechanization. Since 1940 the number of farm tractors has increased almost 200 per cent, motor trucks about 150 per cent, milking machines more than 300 per cent, grain combines 400 per cent, and cornpickers 480 per cent. Including about five million head of horses and mules, farmers now have 80 per cent more farm power and machinery than at the beginning of 1940.

48

istence. A look behind the scene will reveal that wherever there is eroded soil, there will be eroded family life, community life, educational life, church life—and eroded souls.

INCREASING DEMAND UPON THE TIME OF RURAL PEOPLE

Rural church leaders are constantly aware of the fact that

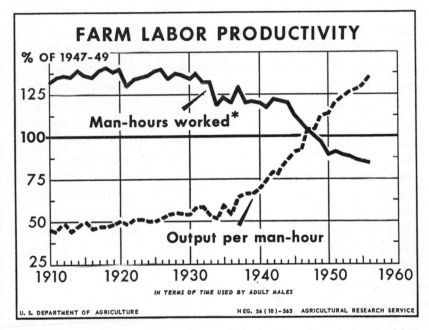

FIGURE VII. Output per man-hour of farm labor has about doubled since 1940. This increase in productivity has resulted both from greater output and from fewer man-hours of work. Production per acre of cropland and per unit of breeding livestock has also gone up, but less rapidly. In 1956, production of crops is almost 25 per cent above 1940 with only 2 per cent increase in acreage of cropland. About two fifths more livestock and products are being obtained with only 10 per cent more units of breeding livestock.

49

the membership of the church must share its time with a multitude of other things. Farm organizations, extension programs, youth groups, informal social groups, are taking the time of rural people which was once devoted to the work of the church. No longer is the church the center of the entire social life of the individual, but it must compete with many other things in the lives of people of a community. This means that church leaders must think through more clearly the place of the church, the function of the church, and the adequacy of the program of the church to meet the needs of people in a community. It means the program of the church must be respectably sound, and the ministry adequate to demand a following in the rural community. With the increasing of professional services in agricultural areas, such as extension agents, youth leaders, conservation specialists, and with the rise of the general educational level of rural people, the church must not be guilty of sending the poorly trained pastor to minister to the spiritual life of the people. Rural dwellers will give an equitable amount of their time to the work of the church when the work of the church can demand their respect.

EXPANSION OF THE RURAL NEIGHBORHOOD AND COMMUNITY

With the increase in good roads and automobiles has come the expansion of the size of a neighborhood and community. The technical definitions of neighborhood and community have been treated in Chapter I. Here it is sufficient to point out that whereas four decades ago a community was usually five to ten miles in diameter, now it is next to impossible to actually delineate a community in size. This expansion has made for peculiar patterns of church loyalties with families traveling past existing

50

churches of their own denomination to churches in towns where they feel there may be better advantages for their children. It has left some neighborhood rural churches struggling with a feeling of defeat and yet a desire for tradition's sake to hold onto the place which has been the center of faith for 50 to 150 years. It means a crisscrossing of community family relation patterns. It means the breaking of old trade loyalties and the development of new. It means the mixing of young people with young people of different neighborhoods as they all travel daily to the town by bus to attend elementary and high school.

INCREASE IN THE LEVEL OF LIVING OF RURAL PEOPLE

Rural living is constantly undergoing changes in the rise of the level of living. Through the vast expansion of electricity to rural people (now available to 94 per cent of the rural homes of America) have come automatic heating, refrigeration, running water, radio, television, power processing of farm products, power milking, and the hundreds of electrical appliances to lighten the burden of the daily household chores. In the brief time of nineteen years, between 1935 and 1954, electrical service grew from 11 per cent of farms having electricity to 94 per cent. Probably no single factor in raising the level of living of farm people has contributed as much as has this service. During the period from 1945 to 1954 the level of living of rural people rose in practically every county in the nation.[5]

THE INCREASE IN EMPHASIS
UPON THE IMPORTANCE OF FARMING AS AN OCCUPATION

Since the establishment of land-grant colleges and the inauguration of the extension service of the college, there has been an increasing importance placed upon the value of farm life as an occupation. The vocational agriculture and home economics program in high schools and the 4-H Club movement have given to rural youth a sense of pride and value of rural life. The extension program and conservation service localized in the county have aided the farmer to use his land more wisely, to increase his production, and hence his profits. Planned farming has been the salvation of thousands of farmers in our nation. Technical knowledge in agriculture and the expanding of agricultural economics to the common man, have increased the efficiency of the farmer, and put farming in the category of business rather than a slipshod way of making a living. The term "agribusiness" has entered the vocabulary of the farmer.

This trend leads more and more young people into the desire to make farming their lifelong profession. Modern housing, electrification, and mechanization have taken the drudgery out of farming and cast about it an increasing sense of security. The fact must be faced, however, that such ideal farming comes with a price. It takes large investments to have modern housing, to mechanize a farm, to stock a farm adequately, and to secure the land. Many young people who wish to enter farming as a life profession are confronted with the cold fact that they are not able to secure the financial backing to make the initial investment necessary to begin. Rather than go through the long process of "climbing the agricultural ladder," they seek outside employment beyond their home community only to become involved in a business or profession for which they have never been trained or intended to follow. There are thousands of trained agriculturists in the business world who desire to someday fulfill their ambitions to become farmers but who will never realize these ambitions. Church leaders must consciously plan ways and means of assisting young people to become established on the land.

ALL TRENDS ARE NOT BAD

One may gain the feeling from this discussion that all trends in rural America are bad. There are two sides to the story. Some of the trends can be fatal to rural life, the church, and even our Christian democracy. But thinking people should be able to examine trends and adjust to meet the changing situation, taking advantage of those elements which can prove an asset rather than a liability.

For instance, take the matter of the expanding community. With good roads and automobile travel, a rural minister is able to serve many more families than was possible under handicaps of poor roads and horse travel. People can travel farther to church. Members of a congregation can get together more often for a well-rounded church program. Co-operation between churches of a given area is possible where once it was impossible.

The blending of rural and urban influences can be fatal to Christian democracy, but it can also be a blessing to it. The naturally conservative rural man may become more liberal in his outlook, embracing better farm practices and conservation measures, developing for himself a more comfortable living, and willing to accept modern techniques of church administration. His children, migrating to the city, can help to maintain a spirit of simplicity and moral integrity in the masses of urban dwellers, assuming their role as church laymen and leaders.

But the one question which stands out above all other remains. Will we as church leaders recognize the value of rural life, the necessity for providing an adequate rural ministry, the absolute necessity of studying and developing a program for the rural church that will challenge the mind of rural people and be a loyal witness for the Christian faith?

To examine trends is one thing; to prescribe an adequate pro-

53

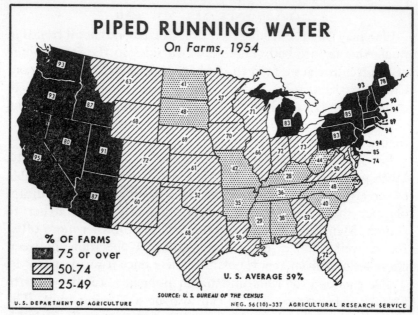

FIGURE VIII. By 1956 64 per cent of all farm families in the United States enjoyed running water in the homes, 74 per cent owned automobiles, 94 per cent had electricity, and 52 per cent had telephones.

gram of church administration to meet those trends, another. The church of the living Christ must not fail to be a witness and source of spiritual life in days of great change to the 61,000,000 people who make up the population of rural America. Behind facts and figures, statistical studies, research projects, charts, maps, and graphs, there are teeming millions who as citizens of a great land, are looking up to, waiting for, praying for, and believing in a church which will not fail. The time has come; the church must "serve to survive." It is the burden of this writing to prove that one of the strongest solutions to the prob-

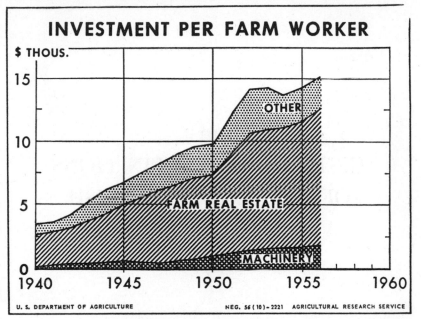

FIGURE IX. As use of purchased resources has increased, the number of farm workers has declined, and the resources available to each farm worker have risen. The value of resources per farm worker varies widely by farming areas. The investment per worker on typical family-commercial cash grain farms in the Corn Belt was about $59,000 per worker in 1956 compared with around $19,000 in 1940. On family-commercial cotton farms in the Southern Piedmont, investment per worker was about $8,000 in 1956, and $2,000 in 1940.

lcms of the rural church is an effective type of church co-operation between congregations in the rural community and the enlarged community. The day is long past when a congregation can exist as an isolated unit. It must co-operate. Town churches are duty bound to serve the whole community. We have reached the stage where we must discover a strategy for survival.

55

III

HISTORY AND DEFINITIONS
OF THE LARGER PARISH
AND GROUP MINISTRY

Through the present century there have been many movements in the direction of co-operation among churches in town
and country areas. These have taken the form of the rural
circuit, the yoke-field, the federated church, the larger parish,
the denominational group ministry, and the county council.
The trends in rural areas have forced churches to co-operate for
survival. In some sections of the nation competition among denominations is still defeating the progressive movement of the
church. The time is far past for a more clearly defined method
of co-operation among rural churches to be "spelled out" for
church leaders. This chapter deals with group organization and
structure within a tangible framework for co-operation of
churches of one denomination or of several denominations.

56

The simplest definition of co-operative church enterprises is: churches within a geographic area co-operating in the several phases of church administration for a more effective program of kingdom advancement.

This definition sets out first a given geographic region. This will be considered in the light of the sociological units presented in Chapter I—the rural neighborhood, the rural community, the enlarged rural community.

The churches within such a region, whether of one denomination or several, are called upon to enlarge their vision of service through co-operation. The major purpose is not to simply build a larger congregation, but to reach all the people within the region with an effective program of kingdom advancement.

THE LARGER PARISH MOVEMENT

Since about 1912 the term "larger parish" has been used with a number of implications. Denominational leaders differ greatly in defining the larger parish. In some areas of the nation it always refers to an interdenominational co-operative work with a closely integrated staff of specialized workers. In other areas, it is nothing more than a denominational "circuit." Or it might be a yoke-field with one pastor serving two or more churches of different denominations. In order to clarify terms and to give something of the spirit behind the larger parish movement, a brief history of the movement is reviewed.

No chronological history of the larger parish movement has been written, although several pieces of literature dealing with the subject piece together something of the background.[1]

The term "larger parish" is commonly attributed for its origin to Harlow S. Mills, who developed such a parish around the town of Benzonia, Michigan, in 1910. The vision of the larger parish can best be told by Mills himself. An entire chapter is quoted from his own account so the reader may be able to catch something of the divine insights, spirit of the movement, and background out of which it was born.

The genesis of a vision is always interesting, though often obscure. On one day a certain side of life is a blank. There is no outlook, no hint of the coming brightness. On another day that side of life is made all radiant and glorious by a vision, clear and definite, that beckons on to future achievement. Sometimes it comes suddenly, like Peter's vision when he was upon the housetop in Joppa; and sometimes it dawns gradually, and little by little paints itself in beautiful colors upon the sky of one's inner consciousness. As remarked in a previous chapter, a conviction is the egg from which the vision comes; but the egg is only dead and formless matter until it is brooded over and warmed into life. So a conviction may be strong and positive, but it may exist for a long time, formless, lifeless, and useless, until it is quickened into vitality by the brooding spirit of a man, and thus becomes an active and inspiring force. So it may be profitable and necessary to the proper understanding of this story to tell how the vision came.

For fifteen years I had been working away in my country parish. They had been happy years of glad, harmonious work. I was satisfied with my job. Though remote from the great centers of population, in a small village, and with people of very modest means, that restless feeling that spoils the preacher and mars the work of so many ministers had been absent. My people were of the strong and sturdy sort, faithful and appreciative beyond many, ready to coöperate in carrying out any plans of work that the pastor might propose. They were splendid followers, responding quickly to all my suggestions. There was a good understanding between myself and the people.

I was called to pass through deep affliction. My home was broken up by a sudden stroke and I was left alone. Into the dark valley of sorrow my people accompanied me as far as they were able to go, and the effect seemed to be to unite us with bonds that were very strong and tender. Every home in all the parish was mine. All the children belonged to me. There was a chair for me at every fireside and a plate at every table.

But as the years went by there came some tempting opportunities to engage in work elsewhere. I was not without my ambitions and aspirations. I wanted to fill out the full measure of my ability and do my best work. And when some opportunities came that made the little country parish seem by comparison rather small and meager, I was not altogether proof against them. To become assistant pastor in a famous church in a large city—to take up the work of general missionary for a whole state seemed to promise fields of usefulness so rich and large that they made a strong appeal to the best there was in me, and perhaps also to the worst. I spent some weeks and months in considering these propositions and finally turned them down. I could not bring myself to sever my connection with those to whom I had been so long and so closely related. The personal tie was too strong and I decided to remain with my people.

With the decision came a thorough heart-searching. It marked a turning-point in my spiritual history. I was impressed with the thought that if it was God's will that I should remain in my present work, it must be for a special purpose. Things could not be in the future as they had been in the past. It would be criminal to turn down a larger work for one that was small unless there were good and sufficient reasons for doing so. If it was the Lord's will that I should remain in that country parish, there must be some work there that it was worth while for me to do, some work that in a proper degree, at least, would approach in importance the larger proposition made by the city and the state. What was the work? Was there anything to be done among those hills and in those rapidly disappearing forests that could fire a man's ambitions and satisfy his high aspirations?

Just here the vision came. At first a whole township was revealed as a possible parish, with every family tributary to the church, and the church performing a valuable ministry for them all. The vision expanded until it took in another township, and parts of three or four more. It became plain that almost half a county was tributary to the church, that five hundred families and twenty-five hundred people were waiting for its ministry. It dawned upon my mental vision that I was called upon to be the pastor of all these people, for five or six miles in every direction, that the Benzonia church was responsible for them all, that they had a right to look to us for service and help, and that if we failed to give it we should be unfaithful to our Master and recreant to our trust. Then I said: "Here is something worth doing. Here may be wrought out an experiment in country evangelization and rural betterment that may help to arrest the downward trend that has become so alarming in these latter days. It was for this that God has kept me here. If I can make this vision a reality, I need not pine for a larger field. If I can help others to see the vision, and inspire them with enthusiasm to make it real in larger fields than mine, and in many parts of our country, I shall never regret that I stayed by the stuff." The vision came as a compensation. It was the reward that God gave for following his leading along those ways where natural inclinations would not have disposed me to go. God wants us to do our best and largest work. He never calls us to a smaller work. If he bids us walk along a humble path and go in an obscure way, we shall find our true life-work there.

The church had for many years been much interested in both home and foreign missions. I preached frequently upon the subject and kept it constantly before the people. Regular collections were taken for missionary objects, and the Every Member Canvass plan had long been in operation. The response was always general and liberal. In fact, those who were well acquainted with the churches of the state have often said that in proportion to its resources, its gifts were larger than those of any other church. Not only did they give money, but they also gave their sons and daughters to carry the gospel to less favored regions. Many of the young women of the church had gone to teach in home mission schools. And there came a beautiful summer Sabbath when a favorite niece, brought up in my home, and an active and useful member of the church, beloved by all, with solemn services in the little church on the hilltop was consecrated to the foreign work and sent forth with the prayers and blessings of all the people to represent them among the awakening millions of China.

As I was sitting in my study one day pondering upon these things, the absurdity of the situation came over me all at once. "Here we are gathering money to send our sons and daughters to the distant parts of the earth, but we are doing absolutely nothing for scores of families that are almost within the sound of our church-bell. We feel some responsibility for the millions of people of other lands whom we have never seen, and never shall see, but we have not felt very much responsibility for those who are separated from us by only a few miles. We are anxious to give the gospel to the colored people, the Chinese, and to those of alien races; but we have felt no such anxiety for those of our own race who are not so very far away. There are many families and hundreds of people within five or six miles of our church that are practically without the gospel, as truly as are the Chinese or the South Sea Islanders. We have made no systematic effort to interest them in these things. We have given them no reason to believe that we are drawn out toward them with Christlike motives. Surely there must be something wrong in our calculations." Then I heard the Master say, "These ye ought to have done, and not to have left the other undone."

And then came the vision of "The Larger Parish." I saw the church reaching out its hand and touching tenderly but effectively all the people in the surrounding country. I saw the church feeling some responsibility for every family, and counting them all as within the bounds of its parish. I saw every family in all that wide region as tributary to the church. I saw the church making systematic plans to carry the gospel to all these outlying neighborhoods. I began to think of all those people as my parishioners as truly as were those who lived near the church and were members of it. And so the vision dawned upon me of the Larger Parish. In my own mind I annexed all the surrounding country and began to make plans for the evangelization and helping of all the people who dwelt therein. So under the stimulus of foreign missions the vision came of the work that should be done and could be done nearer home.

And it may be well to add that since the work of the Larger Parish began, the contributions to foreign missions have more than doubled. There are those all over this wide territory who knew little and cared less about missions three years ago, but who now are eager to make some contribution to the support of the missionary in China, half of whose salary our Church is pledged to provide.

And so the vision came, from above as all good visions do, but it came while walking in the pathway of duty, in the unfolding of a larger experience. He who follows the dawning light will see the vision.[2]

The vision of Harlow S. Mills consisted of five convictions: (1) "The real object of the church is to serve people, and its claim for support should rest upon the same ground upon which every other institution bases its claim for support—that it gives value received." (2) "The church must serve *all* people" within a given geographic area. (3) ". . . it [the church] must serve *all* the interests of the people." (4) ". . . the village church, if it would fulfill its mission, must be responsible for the country evangelization." (5) ". . . if the village church would fulfill its mission, it must be a community church." [3]

The above five "visions" may sound quite obvious to the present-day church administrators, but in Mills's day they were revolutionary. The philosophy undergirding the larger parish was: the central or town church should share its resources of leadership, pastor, and finances with the entire countryside in order that the total population could be affected for the cause of the Christian faith. No individual was to be left out of the responsibility of the church. No individual needs were to be ignored. This meant that if the needs were physical, they became the church's responsibility. If the need was for a better agriculture, this was the task of the church. Mills felt that the church must be thrown upon its own. It deserved support only if it rendered value received.

They [the people] have considered the church as a divine institution, and that because of its divine origin and sacred character it can properly demand respect and support. There was a time in the not very distant past when the ministers of the church, as its representatives, might demand reverence and respect because of the position they occupied. There was much of reverence and regard for "the cloth." But, those days are past. Now the church is valued only for what it does. If it does nothing, it need no longer look for respectful recognition. If it makes no contribution to the community whose value can be seen and appreciated, it cannot expect support or favorable regard. People do not care very much for "clerical dignity." They are not asking what place a man occupies, or what kind of clothes he wears, but what he does for the community. Is he rendering valuable service? They are quite ready to pay for service that is of real worth, but for dignity and traditionary sanctity they have slight regard.[4]

With the above convictions and visions in mind, Mills set out on his new adventure. He made a survey of the parish area on foot. He visited all the families, lived with them, and came to know them. This tour took three months and, according to his own statement, accomplished more than his previous fifteen years of work. He told the people of his vision of a "larger parish," preached on Sunday, talked about it at prayer meetings. He began holding services in schoolhouses in the area. A helper was added to his efforts, providing the "staff" idea for a larger parish. The assistant held services in seven neighborhoods, preaching every Sunday at Grace Church near Benzonia, and as often as he could at other churches. After the first assistant left, two assistants were added, and the parish was divided into three areas. There were twelve places where Sunday services were held. They were arranged so that few families had to go more than half a mile to church. On Mondays the pastors met, talked over their work, and made plans. Needless to say, success in many areas was forthcoming.

With the death of Mills, the parish program disintegrated. This is a clear indication that the program was built around a man rather than the laity. It had however won its way, and the visions of Harlow S. Mills have been the inspiration for hundreds of churchmen in America.

In summary, Mills believed the village church must belong to the rural people and be in close touch with them. It must minister to all the people. It must recognize its obligation to the needs of the people in the area. The only village church which will continue is that one fortified with a strong work in the surrounding area. The lack of teamwork and co-operation makes for weakness.

Contemporary with Mills was Clair W. Adams, in Bement, Illinois. Adams developed a parish which functioned from 1905 to 1912. He ministered to six outstations which were, in modern terminology, federated churches. During the last four years of the parish there was a woman-assistant devoting full time. The program touched every phase of life: social, religious, educational, recreational. Classes in agriculture were held; women's clubs organized; missionary societies started; recreation groups formed.[5]

Warren K. Wilson, rural church secretary of the Presbyterian Board of National Missions, was attracted by the demonstration parishes here and there throughout the country. Most of these were financed through the home mission boards of co-operating denominations supplying funds for equipment and personnel. They were to demonstrate what a church enterprise can accomplish in a given community when furnished with everything needed for work.[6]

In about 1920, Malcolm Dana, director of the Congregational Church Extension Board, began to popularize the term "larger parish." He assisted in establishing several parishes and prepared a sixty-three-page booklet entitled *The Larger Parish Plan*.[7] Harlow S. Mills had given vision to the larger parish. Malcolm Dana gave the larger parish form and systematic organization. He discussed the various types of parishes, the philosophy behind the movement, steps in organizing the parish, the function of a staff of specialized workers, and the place of a lay council. He discussed the larger parish program, the equipment, and how to operate the parish. Included in the work were examples of parishes and a sample constitution.

By 1925, a sufficient number of larger parishes were established to warrant the expenditure of funds for a study of the larger parish situation. Edmund deS. Brunner, employed by the Institute of Social and Religious Research, made the study. His findings were published in a book entitled *The Larger Parish, a Movement or an Enthusiasm?* [8] Brunner found only eighty-four larger parishes, though several hundred were reported to be in existence. The skeptical title of his book reveals the uncertainty about the movement.

Perhaps the greatest contributions made by Brunner's study

were the nine criteria for a successful larger parish. These criteria were delineated out of the reports of the larger parishes studied. They have become the basis for continued exploration in the larger parish field. These are:

1. The territory included is an economic and/or social unit.
2. The territory has adequate resources, under normal economic conditions, sooner or later to support the larger parish.
3. The churches of the parish combine their finances, at least as regards the salary of the staff and preferably for all items.
4. The staff consists of two or more persons with special training or interest in the field of responsibility to which each is assigned.
5. There is a functioning parish council.
6. The parish gives, or at least sincerely aims to give, many-sided service to the whole territory it serves and to every person within it.
7. The parish has exclusive possession of its field so far as Protestant work is concerned, or at least has coöperative relations with other religious groups and with community organizations.
8. The parish recognizes its interdenominational obligations.
9. The parish is assured of the continued support of the denomination or denominations concerned regardless of changes in administrative personnel.[9]

It will be readily seen that the basic assumptions of Brunner are difficult to attain in modern denominational competition, but with modifications, the criteria can stand upon their own merit as sound.

Brunner's own summation of his work merits quoting:

The rural church in the United States could benefit by the impetus and the hope of a new idea. At present the larger parish plan is the only such idea on the horizon. But the larger parish movement is in a state of unstable equilibrium. It has failed so often in one large denomination as to be coming into ill-repute, although such failure was invited. It has succeeded so often as to offer real hope in a discouraging field of religious effort. . . . The future of the larger parish movement is as yet uncertain. It is indeed an enthusiasm more than a movement; but the proper sort of enthusiasm, if it faces and uses the facts, and is linked to social intelligence and knowledge, may set in motion a larger parish movement that will realize the potential contribution of the idea to the religious life of rural America.[10]

Contemporary with Dana was Mark A. Dawber. While serving a four-point rural circuit in Wyoming Valley, Pennsylvania, Dawber tried the philosophy of the larger parish. He began weekly meetings of the whole parish. His program gave new life to the entire area. Mark Dawber has become known throughout the nation for his outstanding contribution as professor at Boston Theological Seminary, denominational executive for the Board of Home Missions of the Methodist Episcopal Church, executive in the Federal Council of Churches of Christ in America before its reorganization, and for his widespread publications in the field of the rural church. His most widely known publication is *Rebuilding Rural America*. [11]

In 1939, the New York State College of Agriculture produced a bulletin entitled *The Larger Parish, an Effective Organization for Rural Churches*.[12] This bulletin was a condensation of the findings from a doctoral dissertation by Mark Rich. Three larger parishes were the basis of the study. The entire scope of the larger parish movement was surveyed. The bulletin had a widespread circulation and did much to foster the larger parish movement. Rich states, "A Larger Parish is a group of churches in a large community or a potential religious community, working together through a larger parish council and a larger parish staff to serve the people of the area with a diversified ministry." [13] An examination of this statement reveals three fundamental ideas in the conception of a larger parish: (1) the community, (2)

67

bona fide interchurch co-operation, and (3) a specialization in training and service among the professional leaders.

THE GROUP MINISTRY

In November, 1937, Aaron H. Rapking assumed duties as superintendent of the department of town and country work of the Board of Missions of the Methodist Episcopal Church in Philadelphia. Rapking had been for sixteen years extension sociologist for the College of Agriculture in West Virginia, and felt keenly the need for bringing the community and church together in a close working relationship. Rapking states:

Soon after I got to Philadelphia, I began to gather such information as I could about the larger parishes. Dr. Jay Stowell, director of Publicity for the Board of Missions worked with me. We decided, on the basis of the knowledge available, to make a moving picture film. Dr. Stowell started out with his camera to take pictures and discovered there was a serious weakness in the program. We discovered that the most of the parishes were highly subsidized by the mission boards. In one situation, our church made $25,000 available over a period of ten years. I came to the conclusion that the major weakness of the program was the fact that the emphasis placed on the importance of the staff tended to bring a somewhat unrealistic relationship between the churches and the staff. That is one reason it seemed wise to me to start with the ministers and laymen involved. Back of my thinking was the conviction that we would have to give the laymen a much larger place in promoting the Kingdom of God building projects in meeting their needs.[14]

In his autobiography[15] Rapking documents the beginning of the group ministry idea.

On September 18, 19, 1938, the following leaders, members of the Board, and others interested met in my office to discuss the future

68

program and policies of the department. E. D. Kohlstedt, Jay S. Stowell, W. A. C. Hughes, Ezra M. Cox, Paul L. Vogt, George M. Bell, A. W. Witwer, J. B. Hawk, Benson Y. Landis, Miss Marian V. Ristine, and Mrs. A. H. Rapking.

This group, after several hours of discussion, approved "The Group Ministry" plan and the "Conference Town and Country Commission" as two of the major phases of the program. Some factors that entered into the discussion were these. Due to modern transportation and communication facilities and economic and social factors, our town and country communities had been for some time in a state of transition. New thought and behavior patterns were being established. In fact, many of the old patterns had faded out of the picture and others had taken or were in the process of taking their places. The individual will always be the first unit in the mind of God and in the process of redemption, but it was becoming quite clear that the individual could not be saved without being saved in relationships. The time was here when an individualistic ministry alone was quite inadequate in grappling with organized crime, neighborhood and community, and world tendencies toward the secularization of life.

In many town and country areas that have the same major trading, recreational, educational, and cultural centers there are from three to six Methodist ministers and from twelve to twenty-four churches.

Here is a word picture of my basic conception of the Group Ministry that I presented to the group: The appointment of our ministers to a regular charge in a recognized natural area such as a county seat town or trade center surrounded by communities and neighborhoods with the understanding that while they would do the work of a good minister of Jesus Christ on their charge, they would also work with other character building organizations to study and promote certain activities in the interest of coming to grips with the problems, the needs and opportunities of the people and thus help bring the Kingdom of God's ideals and attitudes into action in

69

the total life of the area. One minister in the group might be strong in evangelism; another in dealing with people; while another's specialty might be that of promoting the redemptive process through Christian education. These ministers would meet every two weeks and with a map of the territory before them, study, pray, and plan to promote those projects and grapple with those problems, the solution of which would mean much to the building of the Kingdom of God in the area and in the world.

As there is need for ministers to work together in a community or natural area, so there is great need for laymen and churches to join hands and work together to combat evil, promote, strengthen, and make more effective the program of the churches in the area. The establishing of a Methodist Fellowship Council did not call for a change in the present local or district church set-up. The council would be established by electing one man, one woman, and one young person under twenty-four years of age from each church cooperating. The council should meet at least four times a year. The ministers would be members of the council. Committees on surveys, evangelism, Christian education, music, plays and pageants, stewardship, recreation, cooperation with other agencies could be appointed as needed.

In October, 1938, I wrote an eighteen page bulletin, *The Group Ministry Plan*. In this bulletin I suggested projects and activities that could be promoted by the committee. *The Group Ministry Plan* bulletin was designed to help church leaders, ministers and laymen get a clearer picture and fuller realization of the program Jesus had in mind as we pray "Thy Kingdom Come, Thy will be done on earth as in heaven."

In 1950 Glenn F. Sanford became Director of Town and Country Work of the Division of National Missions, The Methodist Church. Sanford had been secretary of town and country work in the North Arkansas Conference for a number of years, and had been an ardent promoter of the group ministry. At one time an entire year was devoted to discovering natural areas for the group ministry, and assisting in setting up programs throughout the conference.

The group ministry became one of the chief objects of Sanford's work in the department of town and country work. Throughout the United States Sanford has been instrumental in establishing group ministries and teaching the philosophy to thousands of ministers and laymen. His pamphlet on the subject has had a widespread circulation.[16]

Sanford has stressed throughout his work the importance of the natural sociological area, or the enlarged rural community as defined in this work. He has emphasized the voluntary aspects of ministers and laymen working together. He has minimized the importance of a constitution, and closely organized program, adapting the "subdistrict" idea as the unit of operation as it is found in The Methodist Church.

There is no question that the group ministry plan of The Methodist Church has preserved many of the original ideas of the larger parish, and in the framework of connectional Methodism, has devised a program of importance for the denomination. Many Methodist leaders feel the group ministry plan holds the secret of success for the work of the church in town and country areas.

The *Discipline of The Methodist Church*, 1956 edition, paragraph 2030, defines a larger parish and group ministry as follows:

The *larger parish* is usually organized with one minister as chairman. He directs the work of a staff of specilized workers. The parish is guided by a council made up of representatives elected by the cooperating churches. The purpose of the larger parish is to serve effectively the entire constituency of the area through the sharing of leadership, resources, and information. This sharing can greatly aid the work of the church in a given community or group of communities. The larger parish may be either denominational or interdenominational.

The group ministry is a voluntary plan of co-operation and association of churches in a natural geographic or political area to make better use of ministerial and lay leaders. A council composed of ministerial and lay representatives from each church is the usual form of organization. This ministry may be organized either denominationally or interdenominationally.

Henry S. Randolph and Alice Maloney of the Presbyterian Church, U. S. A., have in their book, A Manual for Town and Country Churches, a chapter entitled "Organization and Administration of the Larger Parish." [17] A description is given of the larger parish, the function of the parish council, and the organizational work of a parish.[18]

In recent years the trend has been toward denominational emphasis rather than interdenominational co-operation. This has resulted in the failure of many interdenominational efforts and the realization by denominational leaders of the necessity of doing a more dynamic work in the rural church. It is much easier for a group of churches of the same denomination to get together than for churches of different denominations. This has caused some leaders to believe the movement should start with one denomination and spread to other denominations rather than wait for complete consensus of support by all denominations. The larger parish had its origin in the North and East. In those areas sectarian isolationism has not been strong for fifty years. Interdenominational co-operation has been a real possibility. In the South denominational competition is prevalent and sectarian groups are flourishing. This makes denominational co-

72

operation extremely difficult, if not impossible in many areas. The co-operative parish idea is challenging the imagination of denominational leaders in the South, but faced with the sectarian mind, they are adapting the idea to their own denominations.

DEFINITIONS

Out of the above discussion and history of the larger parish and group ministry movements, an attempt will be made to define the traditional larger parish and modern co-operative efforts.

The traditional larger parish consisted of:

1. A group of churches of all denominations within a given geographic region worked a co-operative program of church administration.

2. A staff of specialized workers served the total area.

3. A unified budget of all of the churches of the area paid all bills, including salaries of the staff.

4. A lay council was the controlling body for the larger parish. This council employed the staff.

5. A constitution containing controlling bylaws served as a written document, governing the organization and activities of the larger parish.

In general, present-day definitions will range all the way from the traditional definition given above to a very loosely organized denominational pastoral charge or, on an interdenominational basis, nothing more than a ministerial alliance or a county council of churches. Several definitions from recent literature are given to orient the reader to the modern conception of the larger parish and group ministry.

A larger parish is a group of churches within a definite area which organize themselves to cooperate in the task of ministering effectively

73

to all the people within that area. The plan usually calls for a functional or multiple ministry, that is, a staff or group of workers with specialized assignments. The area included should be a natural trade area or sociological community, wherever possible.[19]

A co-operative parish consists of three or more churches belonging to the same denomination located in a larger rural community working together as though they were one congregation with similar purposes to serve all the people of that denomination and those others unreached in the area with a carefully organized and complete program administered by a diversified ministry.[20]

The definition of the larger parish and group ministry given in the *Discipline of The Methodist Church* is stated on page 71.

Keeping the various definitions in mind, the modern group approach to the town and country ministry can be summarized:

(1) A group of churches either of one denomination or several denominations in a given geographic area co-operate in various phases of the work to do more effectively together what they find difficult or impossible to do alone.

(2) The ministers in the area co-operate in various ways, using their specialized talents for the benefit of the entire group.

(3) Specialized staff members are employed as needs and funds present themselves. Such specialized personnel may consist of a woman director of education, youth work, or women's activities. It might be a specialist in evangelism, music, or organization.

(4) There is a council of lay representatives from each local church in the group which meets regularly to assist in planning the total program of the area.

(5) There is a unified budget varying from only a few items such as the support of a parish paper and a few special events

involving all the churches, to the total salaries of all the ministers and staff in the group.

(6) There are variations in the designation of duties by staff members and the method of their support. In some situations each pastor has one or more churches designated as his pastoral charge. He preaches regularly in this charge and derives his support directly from the contributions of the charge. In other cases, the ministers or staff members serve the entire area, rotating on Sundays leading worship services in the several churches of the group. In this case, the staff is supported from a unified budget.

(7) There are various subcommittees in the lay council to promote a stronger church program for the local church and various activities involving the entire area.

Five main types of co-operative programs can be delineated out of the historical development of the movement and in the light of present-day developments:

(1) *The closely integrated interdenominational larger parish* which is characterized by: (a) a group of churches of several denominations co-operating in a given geographic area; (b) a staff of specialized workers serving the entire area; (c) a unified budget out of which all salaries and other expenses are paid; (d) a constitution governing the organization and work of the parish; (e) a lay council which is the controlling body; and (f) a director, elected by the lay council, who is responsible for the administration of the parish.

(2) *The loosely integrated interdenominational larger parish* which is characterized by: (a) a group of churches of several denominations co-operating in a given geographic sector; (b) each minister in the parish serving one or more congregations and being definitely responsible for ministering to his charge; (c) each minister deriving his support from the charge he

serves; (d) a lay council to guide the various co-operative activities; (e) co-operation in various church activities as the major concern; and (f) a chairman of the parish, elected by the ministers or lay council, as the presiding officer at all meetings but having no executive authority.

(3) *The denominational closely integrated larger parish* which is characterized by: (a) a group of churches of the same denomination in co-operation in a given geographic area; (b) a staff of specialized workers serving the entire area; (c) a unified budget out of which all salaries and other expenses are paid; (d) a constitution governing the organization of the parish; (e) a lay council which is the controlling body; and (f) a director elected by the lay council, or appointed by the proper denominational executive, who is responsible for the administration of the parish.

(4) *The loosely integrated denominational larger parish* characterized by: (a) a group of churches of the same denomination in co-operation in a given geographic area; (b) each minister serving one or more churches in the area and being definitely responsible for the administration of the work to this charge; (c) each minister deriving his support from the charge he serves; (d) a lay council to guide the various church activities; (e) co-operation in various church activities as the major concern; and (f) a chairman, elected by the ministers or elected by the lay council as the presiding officer at all meetings.

(5) *The group ministry* characterized by: (a) a group of Methodist churches in co-operation in a given geographic area; (b) each minister serving one or more churches in the area and being definitely responsible for the administration of the work of this charge; (c) each minister deriving his support from the charge he serves; (d) a lay council to guide the various church activities; (e) co-operation in various church activities as the

major concern; and (f) a chairman, elected by the ministers, the council, or appointed by the bishop, as the presiding officer at all meetings.

The term "group ministry" had its origin in Methodist circles, and applies to a type of program of that denomination; however, there is nothing to prohibit other communions from using the term.

In addition to the above five types of organizations, there are many variations. It is the burden of this writing to grasp the principles of church co-operation and present them in such a manner that church leaders will be able to catch the main spirit of the early larger parish and group ministry movement, applying the type of organization locally which is best suited for the situation. No all-inclusive rule can be applied in a nation as diverse as the United States. Racial and cultural backgrounds, density of population, topography, denominational prejudices, density of church population, meaningful sociological groupings, and many other factors enter into the adaptation of one or another type of parish organization.

It should be kept in mind always that the larger parish or group ministry is first a *philosophy of the service* of the rural church to its surrounding area. It is secondly an organization. As the genuine spirit of service grips congregations and ministers, the type of organization can be perfected to meet specific needs. Organization is not enough; it must be perfected with a sincere desire on the part of congregations, ministers, and church officials to develop the church as an instrument of vital service. As pastors of churches of all sizes of neighborhoods and communities recapture the spirit of Harlow S. Mills and his contemporaries, the work of the modern rural church will be revitalized as it revitalizes the religious and community life of the people.

77

IV

STEPS IN ESTABLISHING
A LARGER PARISH
OR GROUP MINISTRY

The desire for co-operation must stem from the mind of the laity. A successful larger parish or group ministry can never be imposed upon a people. Studies have revealed a quick failure where a program of church co-operation was imposed upon a group of lay people without their knowledge of what it was or their desire to have it. A group of enterprising pastors or an energetic church official may see the need for a larger parish or group ministry and rush into its organization without proper groundwork. To do so only spells disaster and an immunization of the people against any such program for years to come.

Church leaders must assume that: (1) laymen are anxious to see the work of their church prosper; (2) laymen are teachable and will undertake the study of the church when given a fair and intelligent opportunity to do so, as they do in other modern movements, such as methods of soil conservation and better agriculture; (3) when laymen see a need and a possible solution, they are willing to experiment with modern methods of church administration.

The rural layman of today is as well informed in the areas of technology, government, international affairs, economics, and politics as is his city cousin. He has learned production methods on a scientific scale which far surpasses the monotony of doing a simple task on the production line in a great American city factory. The modern ruralite knows the cause and effect of market fluctuation, price supports, parity, and production controls. Farmers' organizations claim hundreds of thousands of members across the nation and are a strong voice in lobbying influence in state and federal legislatures. The rural population of America must never be "sold short." But the rural-minded man is like the typical Missourian—he must be shown. He is teachable, but he must be taught. It is at this point that church executives and pastors need to use the utmost patience and care in leading the laity of a local area into the purpose, need for, and operation of a larger parish or group ministry plan. Once a group of laymen see the need, visualize the possibilities, and are instructed in the operation of a program of local church co-operation, they will become enthusiastic supporters. But this takes time. It calls for patience. It is a process which cannot be rushed. Patience on the part of church leaders, however, will pay dividends in the long run.

In the following pages several true examples are given to illustrate how larger parishes and group ministries are started. No one pattern can be followed universally across the nation. A denomination with a congregational form of government will

79

operate differently from one with an episcopal form of government. An interdenominational parish is usually assisted in organization by a state or county council of churches.

A CLOSELY INTEGRATED
INTERDENOMINATIONAL LARGER PARISH

In a northern Missouri county the laymen from two Congregational and two Presbyterian churches felt the need for strengthening their church programs through co-operation. A half-century tradition was in the background since some of the congregations had been yoked together for short periods under leadership of one minister.

In 1948 the laymen from the four congregations made their plans for organizing a larger parish. Two of the congregations had been without a pastor for three years, one for five, and one for twenty-two years! Yet a small, faithful group had held the churches together with Sunday schools and a semblance of organization.

The state superintendent for Congregational churches and the executive secretary for Presbyterian churches, U.S.A., were called in for assistance. Through their guidance an organization was established whereby the four congregations could work together under the leadership of one pastor. A lay council composed of three persons from each congregation was to be the controlling body. The council was responsible for providing a budget, a ministry, and co-operation among the churches.

A minister was called by the council to serve the four congregations. A budget was established providing for salary of the pastor and other items which affected the entire parish. Each congregation was to provide for its own expenses and for supporting its denominational program.

80

Continued guidance has been provided through the years by the denominational representatives and from the extension department of a nearby college and seminary.

By 1950 two of the congregations in the same town, a Congregational and a Presbyterian, felt the need for organic union in the same building. Both church buildings were in a poor state of repair. A unified effort resulted in raising $25,000 cash. Many hours of contributed labor led to the completion of the building. On October 16, 1952, a new church and educational plant were dedicated. As one unites with this church, one is asked to state a choice—Presbyterian or Congregational. Benevolence contributions are divided equally between the two denominations.

The other two church buildings in the parish have been repaired and remodeled, making suitable places of worship.

During the summer months a student from a seminary is employed by the council to assist with conducting worship, vacation church schools, youth work, and general pastoral responsibilities. This is the only time of the year there is a "staff" of workers serving the parish.

There is a budget committee composed of representatives from the co-operating churches who establish the annual combined budget for the parish. This budget allots funds for pastor's salary, travel expense, secretary, summer student help, office expense, the parish paper, and other items necessary to maintain the co-operative program. Each congregation accepts its share of the total parish expense. Each congregation, in addition to the parish expense, supports its own program of benevolences, sexton, church school, youth work, music program, utilities, and building upkeep. Denominational boards, from time to time, have assisted with the support of the summer student help.

81

Monthly meetings are held by the parish council for planning the total program of the parish. Each fifth Sunday the entire parish meets together at one of the co-operating churches. These meetings are inspirational and aid greatly in the co-operative spirit. The offering at the fifth Sunday meeting is placed in the parish treasury.

Many achievements have resulted from the larger parish. Youth groups are organized in each church, choirs aid in worship in each church, the parish has had a trained minister since its beginning, buildings have been made attractive and worshipful, and more than twenty organizations (such as the Boy Scouts) have served in their respective communities for civic and community improvement.

Points to be noted in the establishing of the interdenominational closely integrated larger parish are:

1. For many years there had been some form of interdenominational interaction which had brought some spirit of co-operation between the laymen.

2. The laymen from the churches met together to discuss possible plans for co-operation. Each church had been without pastoral leadership ranging from three to twenty-two years.

3. Denominational executives were asked to give guidance and help in establishing the larger parish.

4. A lay council of representatives from each of the co-operating denominations was organized to be the controlling body of the parish.

5. A unified budget was established to support the ministry in the parish program.

6. Preaching schedules were adopted providing regular services of worship in each church.

7. A trained minister was called to serve the parish.[1]

AN INTERDENOMINATIONAL
LOOSELY INTEGRATED LARGER PARISH

In a mountain region of Tennessee there had been a tradition of strong church work by the Disciples of Christ, Methodists, and Presbyterians for many years. Both the Disciples and the Presbyterians had established boarding high schools in the region which, by 1944, had been dissolved into the public school system. They, however, had left their mark upon the thinking of the people and opened new vistas of learning with progressive ideas for community improvement.

A strong spirit of co-operation was felt among the pastors and congregations of the different denominations. Revival meetings in which all the churches co-operated were frequent. Pulpit exchange assisted in helping the lay people to recognize there were many areas of faith they all held in common.

There was a sense of need for a strong program of Christian education, but due to the weakness of the individual denominations, it was impossible for any one church to meet the need.

Several meetings of the pastors were held, and it was decided that a larger parish would be the answer. Denominational executives were contacted, and all agreed to help. A time was set in the fall of 1945 for the initial meeting. Denominational executives from the three co-operating churches, ministers of the local congregations, and representative laymen from each church were present. Seventeen local churches were represented. The basic principle adopted was "build the local church in the community through serving the people."

Studies of overlapping responsibilities were made by the denominational executives and pastors. It was discovered that some neighborhoods were overchurched, and by comity agreement two competing denominations placed their memberships in the strongest existing denomination, dissolving one church.

By 1956, a group of four Cumberland Presbyterian congregations had joined the parish. By 1958 there were twenty-seven participating churches in the following categories: Methodists, three pastors and nine churches; Disciples of Christ, four pastors and ten churches; Cumberland Presbyterian, one pastor and four churches; Presbyterian, U. S. A., one pastor and four churches. A full-time director of Christian education is employed by the parish at large and works with all congregations. Each minister in the congregation serves his own pastoral charge from which he receives his support.

For two years after the organization of the parish the ministers met for planning. After two years it was felt that more lay participation was needed. A constitution regulating membership in the parish and stating rules and regulations was prepared and adopted. The constitution provided for a lay council to meet each fifth Sunday to assist in planning the total work of the parish. It took time to teach the laymen to assume responsibility, but gradually they grasped the spirit of sharing leadership and have become very active. By 1957 a new constitution was drafted which established a proviso for four adult voting delegates from each church, the pastor of the church, and one young person under twenty-five years of age. The entire council meets twice annually. There is an executive committee composed of the officers and four department heads which meets periodically for planning. The departments are Christian education, church development, community development, and world outreach. A January meeting of the entire council develops the program for the ensuing year.

Once annually, since the beginning of the parish, a two-day meeting for extensive planning is held. Denominational representatives, both on the national and local levels, are present to share leadership.

Each pastor in the parish serves a charge consisting of from one to five congregations. He is responsible for the ministerial leadership of each congregation and derives his support from the charge. There is a co-operative budget shared by all of the charges and supplemented by denominational boards of missions, which is the means of supporting a full-time director of Christian education who works with all of the ministers and congregations in the parish.

The nine pastors serving the twenty-seven churches preach an average of three times each Sunday. One pastor preaches four times. The mountain and hill country area has small neighborhoods in isolated places. People are handicapped by poor roads, lack of transportation, and inertia. A policy has been established of maintaining the little chapels in rural schoolhouses and country churches. The churches affiliated in the larger parish constitute seventy-five per cent of the congregations in the area and have a constituency of about eighty per cent of the total population.

Many areas of accomplishment can be attributed to the larger parish. Some of these are: leadership training schools, rural community institutes, a parish paper mailed to all families, vacation church schools, nutrition studies, a tuberculosis center for convalescents, a youth camp, the Lord's Acre program, and many other advancements.

From this brief analysis the following steps in establishing the parish can be delineated:

1. Interest was created through pulpit exchange, rural meetings, and other co-operative efforts.

2. The ministers of the region met together for fellowship and planning, and were instrumental in beginning the parish.

3. Denominational executives were called for guidance and council.

4. Studies were made by ministers and executives to determine the areas of overlapping responsibilities.

5. A constitution was adopted regulating the organization of the parish.

6. Laymen were used for planning immediately as they caught the vision of the parish organization and potential.[2]

A CLOSELY INTEGRATED
DENOMINATIONAL LARGER PARISH

Six congregations, one in a village and five in the open country, in the "piney woods" of Louisiana, were being served by three pastors. One pastor was devoting full time to three congregations and living on the charge in a village of three hundred people. He occupied the only parsonage in the area. One congregation was served by a student from a college fifty miles away. Two congregations were served by a seminary student 170 miles distant. The congregations served by students felt they were not receiving the time of their pastor that they deserved. Yet to ask the one full-time pastor to serve their churches was to put upon him too large a responsibility.

Assistance was sought in the person of a full-time rural worker supported by the women's organization of the state. Through her interest and attention she was able to win the confidence of the people and suggest solutions to their problems. Various activities were planned involving the entire area. A county-wide ("parish" is the term used for county in Louisiana, but "county" is used here to avoid confusion with "larger parish") school on publicity was held in co-operation with the state extension service. A county-wide recreation program was held. Church activities involving all the churches of one denomination in the area were planned. Such gatherings brought the people of the county together.

In a class in church administration in the seminary, the student-pastor made a study of the county, involving population shifts, age-sex distribution, time series studies of church membership, church-school enrollment and average attendance, mobility of population, and phases of economic life. The various communities and neighborhoods were plotted on a map, showing location of churches and parish areas. This information was valuable in helping local congregations to see the actual situation and needs.

After much planning and thorough publicity, the professor of town and country church from the seminary was invited to visit the county for a series of meetings on the week end. The chairman of the conference town and country commission, the full-time church worker in the state, and the pastors (in consultation with the official boards) set up a schedule. The professor arrived on Friday night. There was a meeting of representatives to discuss the total involvements. Saturday was spent in the following schedule: In the morning there was a meeting of various representatives of the county, including the pastors of the Methodist churches, the county agricultural agent, the director of the soil conservation district, the county home-demonstration agent, the county superintendent of schools, the church officials, and two representatives from the state agricultural college who were conducting a county-wide workshop in recreation, and representatives from the local churches. This meeting was beneficial to all involved. It assisted in clearing the air on various phases of activities and responsibilities of different leaders. It helped to bring an understanding of the types of programs being promoted in the county. It is amazing to discover how much work is being done in a county by different agencies and also how many overlapping areas there are.

At noon different groups lunched together, creating a bond of

87

friendship. The afternoon was devoted to visiting each of the county churches, stopping at key homes in each neighborhood to become acquainted with one or two families. On Saturday night there was a county-wide recreational program which climaxed a workshop being conducted by the agricultural college representatives. The church representatives, including the professor, rural worker, and chairman of the town and country commission, attended and entered into the program. All of these activities and the visitation gave the representatives a sense of belonging to the group and helped them understand more fully the local situation.

On Sunday the chairman of the town and country commission preached in the county-seat church, located in a town of some two thousand population. It is a fairly strong church with a full-time pastorate. The rural worker visited two of the rural churches, and the professor preached in two of the rural churches at 9:30 A.M. and 11 A.M. respectively.

At two-thirty on Sunday afternoon, 150 lay people gathered at the village church for an "interest" meeting. Factual information was presented concerning the county, such as population shifts, church population, natural sociological groupings, and some predictions as to what would be the future trends. The professor addressed the group on the theme, "Some Modern Approaches to Rural Church Administration." Various phases of the larger parish plan, the group ministry, and the total well-rounded program of the local church were discussed. This was followed with a lively discussion from the lay people. The professor was asked to write out a plan for church co-operation in the county.

Upon returning to his office, the professor drew up a plan for co-operation in the county. The plan suggested that the six congregations being served by three pastors be developed into a closely integrated denominational larger parish consisting of: (1) a unified budget to include all salaries and connectional items; (2) a staff of three pastors, consisting of one full-time resident minister who would be director of the parish, and two students from the nearby liberal arts college; and (3) a lay council, consisting of representatives from each local church. A preaching schedule would be designed so that the director would be in each church at least once each month. The student pastors would rotate preaching in each church. Weekly meetings were suggested for ministers to plan their work, and monthly meetings for the lay council. This plan was duplicated and given wide circulation.

Several weeks after the meetings described above, a group of representative laymen from the six churches met together and planned a parish program. They drew up a preaching schedule for the three ministers. They established a budget and suggested the amounts to be paid by each local church. This plan was taken to the district superintendent by the laymen, accepted by the superintendent, and adopted by the various official boards of the local churches.

The county-seat town of two thousand population had a strong Methodist church. The pastor and laymen of the church had been the stimulus for much of the planning of the work over the whole county. To co-operate with the parish plan, the county-seat church provided funds to assist in employing a secretary for the parish who was responsible for helping with the publication of the parish paper and to assist in office work for the director. Other areas where co-operation was possible for the county to work together were planned.

Several points of procedure are observed in the above illustration:

1. Interest in some type of co-operative action was created

through the patient leadership of pastors, interested laymen, and the state rural worker. This involved two years time.

2. A systematic analysis of the area involved was made. This was simple basic research, consisting of delineating the rural neighborhoods in which there were churches, the rural communities around the central towns, and the enlarged community including the entire county. Additional studies were made of population, changes in population, sizes of churches, organizational structure of churches, and other pertinent data.

3. Professional help was called in from the outside at the time when the mind of the laity was seeking guidance.

4. All avenues were used to assist the professional help to know the situation and to become acquainted with the lay people. They visited local churches, met key laymen, attended Saturday morning meetings, and preached in the Sunday morning services.

5. Plans were presented at the mass meeting.

6. Final plans were made by the laymen and the plans adopted by each local church. Through the whole process no "high pressure" was used by anyone. A simple, slow, and painstaking process of education was used. The significant point is: there was a ground swell among the laymen themselves. This makes for permanency.

A DENOMINATIONAL GROUP MINISTRY

In a midwestern county of 16,000 population, The Methodist Church had twenty-two churches. The county-seat of 2,500 had the strongest church of 700 members. Seven towns, ranging from 250 to 800 population each, had a Methodist church with varying degrees of strength. The remaining fourteen churches were rural neighborhood churches. Most of the open country churches were very weak. Some had not had a regular pastor for several years. Bordering the county were seven open county churches whose neighborhood groups looked to the towns in the major county for their primary services. The churches had traditionally been on circuits involving churches across the county border.

The district superintendent felt a deep concern for the work of the church in the area. He had, fifteen years prior to his superintendency, served as pastor of the county-seat town church. He knew the people over the area and had preached in each of the churches. Through persistent effort the district superintendent was influential in securing support of the area bishop and the General Board of Missions. A commitment of financial aid for support of leadership in a group ministry was forthcoming from the Board of Missions to the amount of $2,700 annually for a period of three years. The area for the group ministry was not a poor farming section but, on the contrary, a comparatively well-to-do area. The problem stemmed from the fact that for many years the small town and open country churches had had poor leadership and for long periods of time, no pastoral leadership at all. It was the faith of the superintendent that if adequate leadership could be found for a period of three years, and a cooperative program be launched for the entire area, the strength of the churches would become such that they would maintain a full-scale, self-supported program within a three-year period.

The ministers of the area were consulted. The county-seat pastor, a man of mature years, pledged support. There were no other trained ministers in the county. Local preachers, or supply pastors as they are called in The Methodist Church, were preaching at several of the other churches.

The assistance of a seminary-trained minister was sought as he was returning from an army chaplaincy. He was supported from funds made available through the resident bishop. For

91

three months an intensive program was conducted. Being a man of untiring energy, dynamic personality, and outstanding preaching ability, he made his way into the life of the people quickly. His technique was simple, yet very effective.

A local church was selected to be the area of work for a week. It was announced in the neighborhood that there would be preaching services at the church each night during the week. Throughout the day a house-to-house canvass was made. Census cards were accurately kept for each neighborhood visited. Each visit, however, was more than simply the collecting of survey data. It was a pastoral call. It became an opportunity for the minister to discover interest in or antagonism to the church, to feel the "religious pulse" of the neighborhood. A hearty invitation was extended to each family to attend evening services at the church.

Existing church rolls (where there were such) were examined. Church officials were visited several times. By the middle of the week it was possible to begin discussion of a progressive program with adequate ministerial leadership if the congregations would do their part. The minister discovered a high degree of suspicion among the laity. They had been promised adequate ministerial leadership before but had been disappointed. It became necessary for the minister to make personal commitments that, if the right kind of leadership could not be found by the Annual Conference, their commitment to the program would not be binding.

Through the type of ministry described above, thirteen churches, to be developed into two pastoral charges, made definite commitments to the financial co-operative program. Other churches of the area and the pastors involved promised support of a group program. At Annual Conference, two seminary-trained men were assigned to the thirteen churches which had been surveyed. Parsonages, though in great need of modernization and repair, were available.

One of the new ministers was named by the bishop as director. It became his duty to give guidance to the denominational program in the entire area. He was to serve as pastor of eight of the congregations. A student from a nearby denominational college was soon called to supplement the preaching schedule on that charge. With the director and student preaching three times, services were held in most of the churches each Sunday.

Regular monthly meetings for the pastors in the group ministry were held. These meetings were in the form of "fellowship and business." A potluck supper was shared by the families of the ministers at one of the homes. After the supper the ministers met for a one-hour business session. The district superintendent would usually attend these meetings—not to preside or dominate, but to share in the total planning process. Additional meetings of the ministers were held during the month for study, planning, or the development of special programs.

A lay council was elected, consisting of one lay representative from each of the eight pastoral charges and five additional lay persons, representing the five major areas of local church emphasis: missions, evangelism, education, finance, and youth work. This lay council met quarterly with the ministers for over-all planning of the work of the group ministry.

By the end of the first year, a growth in every area of the work of the church was felt in all of the churches. Each church had a pastor, though they had, in most cases, to share him with other churches. By the end of the third year there were eight pastors working co-operatively with twenty-nine churches. All mission support was absorbed by the local congregations and salaries were substantially increased. At this writing, twelve years after its beginning, the group ministry continues to operate. Many changes have been made, but the basic structure still prevails.

Points of procedure to be noted from the above case:

1. A denominational executive with a deep concern for the area was instrumental in making the first move toward co-operative action.

2. The interest of the ministers and churches in the area was stimulated through personal contacts.

3. The interest and support of the resident bishop was secured through correspondence and personal contacts.

4. Denominational support was solicited under the condition that proper personnel could be secured, and the local churches promised their share of support. The mission support was to be for three years only.

5. A trained, experienced minister was called to revive interest in the work of the local church, inform the local people of the possibilities of an enlarged program, to make a community canvass, and to set up a temporary program. His work consisted of:

    a) intensive visitation, making a community study
    b) preaching in local churches
    c) discussing the possibilities with interested officials
    d) setting up the program and receiving local church commitments for support

6. Denominational executives remained very close to the project, giving full support where needed.

7. Trained leadership was brought in at the proper time to assume direction of the entire project and to be pastor of some of the churches.

A GROUP MINISTRY

In a heavily populated section of a midwestern state, the pastor of the county-seat church felt the need for extending the work of the church in a much larger scope. The county had, in 1950, a population of 45,000 and the county-seat town, 8,000. It is the largest of five towns in the county, and more than one half of the population is rural farm. It is in a rich farm area with a decided social stratification, consisting of large landowners and many renters or sharecroppers. Through the interest of the county-seat pastor, the other pastors of the county were invited to study the possibilities of a concentrated program in the area. Parish responsibilities were defined, and areas in which there was neglect of pastoral leadership were accepted by one of the ministers.

Monthly meetings of all ministers were planned. Stimulation of interest and concern on the part of the stronger church were created in the neglected areas by the ministers in their group meetings. Surveys were made of the neglected areas. After a few months of co-operation, a full-time rural worker was employed to work in the county. Her salary was paid by the denominational board of missions of her church. The county-seat church bought a car for her use. All churches of the parish shared in the travel expense and room rent for the worker. She was under the direct guidance of the director of the parish who was the pastor of the county-seat church, but she was available for work in any area of the county.

Gradually the membership of the stronger church became more concerned with extending the church to neglected rural areas. They became willing to share their pastor with such areas, permitting him to preach in country churches at early Sunday morning and at midweek services. Several churches were reopened or built as the result of this program. Group co-operation, at the time of this writing, is among the young people, women's groups, laymen's organizations, training programs for Christian education, lay-speaking groups, annual preaching missions, and many other areas. The total life of the church has been greatly stimulated.

Points of procedure to be noted from the above case:

1. The group ministry idea was stimulated by an interested county-seat pastor and a strong congregation.

2. The ministers of the same denomination were invited to discuss the life of the church in the county.

3. Studies were made to determine unreached and neglected areas in the county.

4. Ministers accepted responsibility areas for their special projects.

5. Interest on the part of the local church in the neglected areas was stimulated by the pastor, and support of the congregation to do something was forthcoming.

6. Over-all co-operation made possible the employment of a full-time rural worker for the county.

7. Denominational executives gave leadership when needed.

8. Co-operation by interested groups of the various churches was entered into vigorously.

SUMMARY AND CONCLUSIONS

From the reviews of the five cases above and from additional experience, a general pattern for establishing a group ministry or larger parish is designed:

1. Interest must be stimulated among laymen and ministers as the first step. This is an absolute must, for the total success of a co-operative program is dependent upon the support through sincere co-operation of persons involved. This can be done

through personal contacts, group meetings, visual aids, attendance upon town and country conferences, and reading of literature.

2. A survey of the area must be made to determine natural sociological groupings, population trends, nature of the population, the strength of the church, economic conditions, and any other pertinent data.

3. Full support of denominational executives is necessary.

4. There should be professional or specialized leadership, such as a denominational or interdenominational town and country director, to assist in planning and setting up the program.

5. Lay people should be used throughout all planning.

6. Materials should be presented to lay groups. One of the most effective methods of presenting findings of studies and of creating interest is that of having a meeting of all lay people involved in the area in which the parish or group ministry is to be established. At the appointed time, after careful and thorough planning with repeated meetings of the ministers and various lay groups, have an all-day meeting of laymen at some central point. At the meeting present the findings from the research which has been made. A map of the county should be prepared, showing the location of the churches, natural groupings, such as neighborhoods, communities, and enlarged community boundaries, population of the various sections of the county, and trends in the population. Graphs should be prepared, showing the farm trends, economic trends, health and welfare situations, and other pertinent data. It is advisable to invite certain specialists in the area to make presentations at this meeting. These could be the county agricultural agent, speaking on agricultural trends; the superintendent of schools, speaking on trends in the public school system; the county attorney, speaking on the crime situation in the county; or, the welfare agent, speaking on health

97

and welfare in the county. Such presentations will assist the people to understand their area better and to see the work of the church in the light of the total picture of the county.

At the appropriate time in the meeting, the plan of the group ministry or larger parish can be presented. This should be done in general terms, leaving the specific plans for the area to come from lay group meetings. No attempt should be made to organize at this meeting other than the election of some temporary officers so the efforts of the meeting will not be lost. These officers will then be responsible for carrying the information to the churches involved and assisting to establish a permanent organization.

It must again be stated that the process of group action is usually slow. People do not change their minds quickly and are not willing to accept a new organizational plan without first fully understanding it. Intergroup co-operation is not an effort to manipulate laymen into a program, but to elevate the life of the church in totality within a given geographic area. Careful planning, thorough research, many group meetings, and patience will pay large dividends in establishing a group ministry or larger parish.

THE LARGER PARISH OR
GROUP MINISTRY AT WORK

Many large parishes operate with a constitution as a governing directive which defines the place of the staff, membership churches, conditions of membership, the council, purpose of the parish, name of the parish, and other areas of activity. Some parishes do not have a constitution, though a constitution clarifies responsibilities and assists in the over-all government of the group. There is a general consensus among rural church leaders that a constitution is not needed in a group ministry. A sample constitution is given in Appendix A.

What a larger parish or group ministry does is dependent upon the ingenuity of the staff and council. The program can be as broad or as limited as the co-operating churches will permit. In this chapter suggestions are made for the functioning of the parish in various areas of co-operation. The material is presented purely as suggestive, and by no means is to be considered exhaustive, final, or binding upon an organization.

THE STAFF MEETINGS

Staff meetings consisting of the director, all ministers in the group, specialized workers, and denominational representatives should be held with regularity. The number of meetings per month is somewhat dependent upon the size of the staff and the size of the group. In a closely integrated larger parish staff meetings must be held weekly to keep the total plan of the parish administration in operation. Such a parish is within one community which is usually not more than five to ten miles in diameter, making it possible for the staff to be together often. In a group ministry the organization can be in an enlarged community consisting of all churches within a county, section of a county, or even overlapping into neighboring counties. This may mean the ministers are as many as ten to thirty miles apart. Travel then becomes a problem, and monthly meetings might be the only solution. It is recommended that meetings be held with no less frequency than monthly, and if possible, weekly.

There are three main types of staff meetings: (1) fellowship, (2) business, and (3) study and personal enrichment.

(1) The fellowship meeting is placed first, not by accident, but in order of importance. There is no way a group of ministers can function as a group without the basic element of Christian fellowship. Family relationships in a staff are important. At least monthly all members of the families of the staff should be together for a potluck meal and an opportunity for fellowship with one another. There will no doubt be some who will say, "We do not have time for this type of meeting." The answer is, "You do not have time not to have such a meeting." There is tremendous therapeutic value in breaking bread together. As

members of a staff and their families know one another in informal situations, suspicion is erased, a sense of worth emerges, and group solidarity is formed.

The rural pastorate is often a lonely situation. Pastors are isolated from the fellowship of ministers. It is impossible for the pastor to be too intimate with certain members of the congregation without jealousy arising and his showing partiality in the congregation. Family staff gatherings aid materially in supplying a need for fellowship and intimacy of contacts. Such meetings should be held in homes unless the group is too large. If too large, it can be in one of the churches. The meeting should be for staff only, and does not include lay people of the parish. The ministry is a profession. The wife of a minister is, whether she wants it or not, a part of the ministry. She needs to feel her part in the total life of the parish. She is important. Differences of educational qualifications, cultural backgrounds, and theological interpretations are minimized around the fellowship table.

If the distances between residences are great, a business meeting of the ministers can be combined with a fellowship meeting. After the meal the ministers can find a room for privacy and go into business session for an hour. Wives and children can visit together.

(2) The business sessions should be conducted with a sense of sincerity, earnestness, and democracy. An agenda should be presented by the director with ample opportunity for additional items of business to be presented by the staff, and a definite time of meeting should be scheduled with a stated time of adjournment. The agenda should contain such items as preaching schedules, lay speaker's schedules, special events of the parish, routine emphases within the program of the local church, denominational programs, connectional meetings, committee re-

ports, vacation church schools, special evangelistic programs, and stewardship activities. The work of a larger parish is simply the work of a local church examined by the total staff. There will be points of difficulty within a specific local church to be examined and discussed by the group. All persons should be heard from, if there is any friction or problem.

(3) A third type of meeting which is held by many staffs is for the purpose of study and personal enrichment. All ministers must keep abreast of what is taking place in the various fields related with the ministry. One of the tragedies of the ministry is that so many men become so involved in administration of the church that they neglect the day-by-day study so necessary to a vital preaching ministry. Stated times should be set aside for the staff to get together for study. The stimulation of a group participating in simultaneous examination of a piece of literature can be fruitful. Some book on the Bible, theology, Christian ethics, church history, missions, or other related fields, can be the basis of study for a month or more. Definite assignments can be made by the director or study leader. Each member of the staff should take his turn in directing the discussion. Such study meetings should be held as often as the staff feel they can attend.

THE LAY COUNCIL

The council composed of lay representatives from the co-operating churches is a "must" for a continued progressive program. The lay council is projected for the purpose of creative thought for the total church program of the parish area. By planning together with the staff, a constructive over-all program of church activities can be prepared to reach all churches and people of the area effectively.

The council should be composed of representatives from each

congregation. These can be persons elected because of their position in the local church, such as chairman of the official board, president of the woman's organization, and president of the youth organization. Or the representatives can be elected by the local churches on the basis of their particular qualifications to fit the position.

The council should meet at stated intervals. If the parish is geographically small, a monthly meeting can be held at one of the local churches. If the parish or group ministry is large, meetings should be quarterly. The meetings should be of a business nature to discuss the various phases of local church and parish programs. There should be a definite agenda consisting of reports of committees, discussions of parish events, items presented by the director, finances, and all matters pertaining to denominational programs.

To facilitate the work of the council, committees should be selected for various phases of the work. The committee does not need to be confined to the members of the council, but the chairman of each committee should be a member of the council. Standing committees should be appointed to be responsible for the promotion of work within the local church in the areas of evangelism, education, finance, missions, worship, and social action. These can be standing committees endowed with the responsibility of examining the work of the church in the parish in the various fields, and assisting local churches in promoting strong programs.

In addition to the standing committees, there will be need from time to time for temporary committees to examine such matters as charge boundaries, church location and co-operation, farm and home, co-operation with community agencies, lay speakers, and special events involving the entire parish.

Committees should take their work seriously, examining the phase of church work which is their responsibility, and assisting local churches in perfecting their program in every phase. It may be necessary for the committee to visit local churches to see firsthand their particular phase of work in the church. At all times it should be kept in mind that the major objective is to do the work more efficiently in the local church.

THE EXECUTIVE COMMITTEE

The elected officers of the lay council should meet with the ministerial staff at stated intervals or on call. Such meetings will assist in keeping the total program of the parish in harmony, and will make it possible for the lay representation to express desires and assist in total planning. At such meetings it should be decided by the group who is to preside, the director or the chairman of the lay council. The usual pattern is to authorize the chairman of the lay council to preside.

FINANCING THE LARGER PARISH OR GROUP MINISTRY

The type of financial program of a co-operative program is dependent upon the type of parish or group ministry. If the parish consists of one rural community with its surrounding rural neighborhoods, it is possible to have a completely unified budget. In this case the parish council will draw up a budget consisting of staff salaries, denominational executive salary, connectional items for the denomination or denominations, mission giving, and any other item which affects the total parish. There should be some allowance made for staff travel, office expense, the parish paper, and special parish events. Each church within the parish will accept its proportional share of the budget and pay to a common treasurer who, in turn, will make all payments for the parish. Each local congregation will need a treasurer who will receive funds from the members of the church through their regular contributions. He will make the payments for the congregation to the parish treasurer. Each local congregation will take care of its church-school literature, building maintenance, janitor service, and utilities.

The unified budget has been found to operate very successfully in many larger parishes. Brunner, in his study in 1933, states this to be one of the criteria for a successful parish. The unified budget will work in a small parish where people have one community center and know one another. It is difficult to operate, however, and probably should not be attempted, when two or more rural communities are involved.

In the denominational group ministry, support of the individual staff members, with the exception of a specialized worker who serves the whole area, should come from the charge served by the individual pastors. Each pastor in the group ministry serves one or more congregations. This is his definite responsibility, and he should receive his salary from the churches he serves. In this event, the group ministry as such does not have a large treasury. It will need to have a treasurer who will receive funds from each church to support enterprises involving all of the churches. Supported from this central fund are such items as a parish paper, office expense for the director, the annual parish day, and other co-operative activities. If there is a specialist who serves the total area, such as a deaconess or rural worker, her salary and travel expense should be paid through the common fund.

In an enlarged community consisting of several rural communities, the ties of the people are hardly strong enough to support a closely integrated treasury for all salaries. It is much better to have each minister serve a definite charge and derive his salary from that charge.

CO-OPERATIVE ACTIVITIES
OF A LARGER PARISH OR GROUP MINISTRY

There are many areas of co-operation within a co-operative program. The ingenuity of the group in planning can discover areas beyond this discussion.

The Parish Paper. An essential in a larger parish or group ministry is some type of parish paper, which can take the form of a mimeographed page up to a rather elaborate printed magazine type of publication. Regardless of the actual form, there are several underlying principles which should be observed: (1) The paper should not be on a subscription basis. Support should come from the co-operating churches on the basis of number of families in the church. If there is no central treasury from which such a paper can be supported, it should receive support from the local churches involved. This support can come from an amount set aside in the budget, from the church school, or from individual contributions. The paper will be defeated in its purpose if subscriptions are taken. Any subscription paper will not go to all families. The paper should also be mailed to all constituents of the churches of the parish as a means of cultivating the prospects for church membership. Support is not difficult to obtain after the paper has had two or three issues.

(2) The paper should be mailed from one central office to all families within the membership of the churches of the parish or group ministry. It should be mailed to all prospective families for church membership. Such a list of prospects can be compiled by a careful examination of church-school records, youth activity rolls, women's society rolls, and lists of persons contacted through any organization within the church. Additional members of families who are not members of the church will be discovered. Visitation cards should be carefully kept of persons vis-

106

iting church services. The community house-to-house survey is a source of discovering membership prospects. Any family contacted in any way by the church, or any family without a church home becomes a potential for church membership. These persons should receive the parish paper.

(3) The paper should have a standing column which announces the church service schedules for all congregations, names and addresses of staff members, ministers, and members of the lay council.

(4) The paper should carry articles of general concern for the entire area. It should announce coming events involving all churches and report on events that have taken place. A column should be devoted to the activities of each church, using the names of persons freely in reporting local church activities. There should be space given to denominational programs of a general or church-wide nature. Many readers will not receive the church organ of the denomination, and the parish paper should provide a limited amount of general information. There should be a calendar of coming events or announcements. Articles on timely topics by members of the staff should be published. Sermons, generally, are not very interesting reading.

(5) Someone within the parish, a minister, the director, or a layman, should be appointed by the lay council to be the editor of the paper. The best talent available should be secured for this task. It does take time, but it is one of the efforts which will pay large dividends when well done. The usual news formula of "who, when, where, what, why" can be applied to preparing news articles. News is the reporting of incidents in which people will find interest.

(6) The mechanics of preparing the paper and distributing it must be done by the staff and council. A good mimeographed job has advantages of being more inexpensive than printing.

Stress, however, should be placed on *good*. Care should be taken in cutting stencils, heavy paper should be used, slip-sheeting should be done if necessary, and there should be a uniform distribution of ink. Frequently a small-town printer will prepare the paper in printed form for only a little more cost than mimeographing. Much more material can go into a printed paper than mimeographed. Sixteen pages of double-spaced typed material can be put into four pages of printed matter of the same size. Printing has the added advantage of the use of pictures. Some of the modern lithographing methods of producing copy are quite inexpensive and far superior to mimeographing.

The person responsible for circulating the paper should have resources available for keeping an up-to-date mailing list. This should be in constant revision through the assistance of staff members. Some type of addressing machine should be supplied by the lay council. Mailing can be done with the special postal law and regulation permit for nonprofit organizations which permits mailing at minimum cost per copy.[1]

Activity groups in the parish or group ministry. There are three main activity groups within the structure of the organized church: youth, men, and women. As far as possible each of these groups should be recognized in planning the over-all program of the larger parish or group ministry. If the parish is denominational, the program of the denomination should be used. If interdenominational, the program can assist greatly in interest for the entire area and stimulate a stronger program in the local church.

There should be a youth organization consisting of all young people from each local church. This cannot, except in the case of a very small parish, take the place of local church organizations. Young people enjoy the fellowship of other young people. They enjoy "going places," and will go places when left on their own. A monthly parish meeting of the young people, consisting of periods of worship, study, and recreation will create interest and strengthen the entire Christian cause. Once each year the youth from all churches should have a prolonged program for all youth covering the greater part of three days. Such a program should be in the winter. The young people can meet at the sponsoring church beginning with the evening meal on Friday, continuing through Saturday, and closing with the noon meal Sunday. The program for such a meeting must be well-balanced between worship opportunities, study classes on timely topics, and recreation. The sponsoring church can entertain the young people in homes overnight and through breakfast. Other meals can be provided by the church ladies. A small fee can be charged to take care of expense. Where church building facilities are not adequate, frequently the high school building can be used. The members of the parish staff can be used as speakers, teachers, and recreation leaders. The denominational personnel from connectional offices will be happy to give leadership in such an endeavor.

A strong program of summer camping should be promoted for youth in the parish. Young people can attend their denominational camps but emphasis can be placed upon the camp by the entire group.

The work of the men can be greatly enhanced by periodic meetings of all men from the co-operating churches. The meetings can be held at different churches at stated times. There should be some type of organization of the men placing responsibility in the hands of proper persons for program and planning. Frequently the men's organization becomes the sponsoring agent for a layman's speaking group to supplement worship services in the parish and to speak in local churches on timely subjects. Fellowship can be stimulated by a men's organization, creating splendid worship and learning opportunities.

The work of the women of the parish is usually more clearly defined by denominational women's societies than that of the men. Many small congregations, however, find the denominational organization too complicated to follow. It is difficult to have an active society with five women when the organization calls for sixteen officers. But the five women need the fellowship and strength of the larger organization. Sometimes a small church can organize as a circle of a larger church not too far away. Certain activities can be done together such as business and study sessions or special training classes. The stronger churches can be of great assistance to the smaller churches.

Leadership education. The cry from churches across the nation is constantly for more and better trained church-school leaders and teachers. The larger parish or group ministry provides a means for training of teachers and church leaders by having, annually or twice each year, training classes on a parish-wide basis. It is difficult to secure teachers for leadership classes for the very small congregation, but teachers can be secured for a leadership school in which there are a number of churches cooperating. Transportation facilities make it possible for teachers to travel to such training schools several miles away. Denominational executive secretaries of education will welcome the opportunity to assist in setting up schools and providing teachers. Classes should be conducted in administration of the church school, methods of teaching children, youth and adults, how to use literature, the Bible, church history, theology, and many other subjects relevant to the total teaching-learning process.

The Parish Day. At least annually there should be a parish day, drawing all members of all congregations together for a full day of church activity. The program should be on Sunday and

110

consist of church school for all age groups, morning worship service, a basket dinner, and an afternoon program. Such a day's observance would probably tax the capacity of the largest church building in the area and should be held in some type of open-air pavilion. A special lay council committee will be needed to make the plans. Such plans call for selecting church-school teachers, selecting the speaker for the day, providing the facilities for the meeting, such as tables for the dinner, musical instrument, drinking water, rest rooms, parking grounds and persons to assist in parking cars, hymnbooks, a printed order of service, the program, and choirs. The speaker for such a meeting should be someone brought in for the day. A specialist in the field of town and country work often can be secured for such a meeting. He should be provided with travel, entertainment, and honorarium. Such expenses can be provided for with the offering at the meeting.

The parish day brings a spirit of enthusiasm to the entire constituency. It gives the members of the individual churches an opportunity to meet others in the parish. It gives the parish or group ministry an opportunity to express its strength. Widespread publicity will be given to such a meeting by public press. The parish witnesses as a co-operative program for the Christian cause. It makes an opportunity to bring to the area outstanding national leadership in the field of town and country church. This is not possible for a church working alone, but when resources are pooled, leaders are anxious for the opportunity to participate in such a gathering.

Co-operation with Agencies. There are many agencies working in rural areas for the betterment of the total community life. The county agricultural agent and his assistants, soil conservation service, farmers' organizations, vocational home economics and agricultural departments in high schools, and other persons

111

and organizations are working for the county. The parish staff should know leaders in various fields and be in a position to co-operate with their programs. Staff personnel of various agencies should be invited to assist in parish programs wherever they have a contribution to make.

Simultaneous Action. There is increased strength for the churches if they will do many things at the same time. Vacation church schools, evangelistic campaigns, Lord's Acre programs, visitation programs, and other activities can be strengthened if promoted in all the churches of the parish at the same dates. The staff can plan together how to do the work. Literature can be secured in bulk orders. Publicity can be done together. The psychology of group action will strengthen the total program. If there is a church reluctant to launch into some phase of the work of the church, simultaneous action will encourage its participation.

One of the largest benefits from simultaneous action is that of advertising. Newspapers are anxious to give space to churches. So much material sent to the editor is simply routine announcements that he becomes weary in his effort to be of service to the church. He even looks for the opportunities to publicize any work which is on a broad scale. Publishers are concerned with material which reaches the largest number of their readers. Parish-wide programs are of concern to many people and make for good reading. The church needs to take advantage of all opportunities for good publicity.

An Active Farm and Home Committee. One of the major problems of the rural church is the depletion of population. Young people finish high school and, unable to find a position, must migrate to the larger town or city for gainful employment. There should be a committee in the parish to study the "job opportunity" situation within the area. It would be well for the committee to invite the agricultural extension agent, the local bankers, leading merchants, and agricultural leaders to come together in discussion of methods of providing ways by which young people can secure adequate employment to remain in the community. The 4-H and Future Farmers programs are stimulating many youth with a desire to remain in their community. But, confronted with the necessity of having a large cash outlay to begin farming, they find it impossible to finance the operation and must go on to the city. An active committee in the parish should plan for distribution of literature on father-son farm operating agreements, family farm transfer agreements, and on assisting young people in getting started in small businesses.[2]

Community Outreach. The parish should have an active committee to study the outreach of the community in various phases of social, economic, and health welfare of the people. The committee should make certain investigations using some type of guide to examine the life of the community to see if it is filling needs in the fields of health and welfare, religion, communications, government, education, conservation, recreation, and economics. Wherever the committee finds a deficiency in community life, measures should be taken through co-operation of all agencies to overcome the deficiencies.[3]

Goals for a Larger Parish or Group Ministry. The parish council should think through the objectives of a co-operative program. It is always a good policy to have standards toward which the group is moving. A list of goals is given as suggestive:

1. Worship services in each church at least once each Sunday
2. Vacation church school in each church annually
3. At least annual opportunities for teacher training
4. A program of missionary education in each church, using missionary speakers, visual aids, and classes

113

5. All youth active in their local church and parish programs, summer camps, and midwinter institutes

6. All women of the parish having an opportunity to participate in a woman's organization

7. An active men's program for all men of the parish

8. A strong stewardship program making it possible for the parish to support itself and carry a proportional share of mission work

9. A constructive program of educational, visitation, and mass evangelism in every church

10. The efficient use of such media as newspapers, radio, and television

CONCLUSIONS

A concluding word needs to be said about the larger parish and group ministry. All churches should feel the total responsibility for the work of the whole area involved. Harlow S. Mills was right in his diagnosis of the work of a larger parish. His criteria are repeated for emphasis: (1) "The real objective of the church is to serve people, and its claim for support rests upon the same ground upon which every other institution bases its claim for support—that is, it gives value received." (2) "The church must serve *all* the people" within the parish area. (3) ". . . it [the church] must serve *all* the interests of the people." (4) ". . . the village church, if it would fulfill its mission, must be responsible for the country evangelism." (5) ". . . if the village church would fulfill its mission, it must be a community church." [4]

By a group of churches within a rural community or an enlarged rural community looking seriously at their task of ministering to all of the people and all of the needs of the people within their area, a strong church program can be effected.

Such a co-operative endeavor has brought a spirit of optimism to the discouraged church. Members of a small congregation sense the strength of the whole group. They feel they are not alone. They feel they have a mission to perform. As the churches in a larger parish or group ministry become stronger in every way, they become more attractive to the person who is unchurched, and are able to do a better task of evangelism.

The leadership of a parish must always keep in mind the total life and work of the church in the whole area. It is a group of ministers and a group of congregations working together to minister efficiently to the total constituency of the community.

VI

LEADERSHIP IN A LARGER PARISH
OR GROUP MINISTRY

Leadership roles in any type of group work carry the success or failure of group co-operation.

Studies of larger parishes have revealed that spasmodic successes have been in direct relationship to ability of leaders to maintain harmony, understanding, and co-operation. Brunner found in his study of parishes that the most prevalent cause of failure in parishes was leadership conflicts:

Faulty administration, other than that already noted, of one sort or another, was also an important cause of failure. Methodists seem to have suffered more from this cause than any other denomination. A new bishop, or more often a new district superintendent, came into a supervisory relationship to a larger parish. He was not interested in or informed about the plan, its values, and methods of functioning. He felt that it was taking too much money, energy, or personnel. He

116

placed the parish upon the defensive instead of giving it the moral or financial support formerly forthcoming. In such situations mistakes, dissensions or the like, were magnified and failure resulted. One bishop stated, "There are simply not enough denominational superintendents who understand and believe in the larger parish plan to make it possible to develop parishes, especially interdenominational ones." [1]

To see the problems involved is to seek answers to these problems. This chapter attempts to do three things: (1) define the various leadership roles and to discuss their interrelatedness; (2) describe some of the qualifications of the director of a larger parish or group ministry; and (3) present some fundamentals of leadership to assist a director in his responsibilities.

Volumes have been written on leadership by business administrators, psychologists, educators, and sociologists. It is impossible to treat the subject adequately in this writing; only some fundamentals can be presented. It is hoped that anyone in a leadership role will take advantage of the bibliography on leadership for further study.

DEFINING LEADERSHIP ROLES

Leadership roles in the larger parish and group ministry. There are six major leadership roles to be considered: (1) the director; (2) the ministers making up the staff; (3) the "specialist" worker in the parish employed by the entire parish (In a closely integrated larger parish, two and three will be the same. A typical pattern, however, is for a parish to have a director who is also a pastor, several pastors, and one or more specialized workers, such as a deaconess, director of education, and director of music.); (4) the lay council; (5) the official body of church officers in each local church; (6) the denominational executive (district

117

superintendent, association missionary, synodical director, or regional director of town and country work).

Due to the different types of government in denominations, it is necessary to define roles in terms of episcopal and congregational systems. In the episcopal form of government much authority is in the hands of the denominational executive, the district superintendent. He is close to the churches and ministers in his district, as well as the bishop of the episcopal area. He is a superintendent in every sense of the word and is expected by his denomination to promote the work of the church in the territory under his direction. He is the liaison between the local church, the pastor, and the bishop. It can be readily understood that any discussion of leadership roles must consider the district superintendent in a denomination with an episcopal form of government.

On the other hand, churches using the congregational form of government do not place as much authority in a denominational executive but are more autonomous in the local church. For instance, a district superintendent in The Methodist Church is virtually a part of a parish staff, while a denominational executive in a congregational type church is simply an advisor. The first section of this chapter is, therefore, divided into two areas: (1) a discussion of leadership roles in The Methodist Church, typifying the episcopal form of government; and (2) an investigation of leadership roles in the congregational type of government. Sections two and three are universal in all churches.

The director in a Methodist larger parish or group ministry. The director of a Methodist larger parish or group ministry should be appointed to the office by the bishop after careful consideration by the cabinet. The needs for the office should be considered, and the cabinet should make every effort to find the person best qualified for the office. Too much stress cannot be placed upon the importance of sincere, careful searching to find the right director. No cabinet should take this task lightly.

The best qualified minister available should be considered, even though it could mean transferring a man from another conference to fill the role. If he is a pastor within the group ministry and serving as director, *he should be pastor of the leading charge.* It is difficult for a director to maintain leadership status if he is not in the strongest charge. This appointment should be protected when a change of pastors is necessary.

The director appointed to succeed a parish director should be selected with the same careful consideration as the first director. He should be thoroughly informed about the co-operative work and his responsibilities connected with it. He should be not only "willing" to accept the director's responsibility but "anxious" to accept it. Many Methodist group ministries have failed with changes of leadership simply because the incoming pastor-director accepted his role as pastor but not as director. He felt the larger parish or group ministry was something "tacked on," or was not important.

Within The Methodist Church, the larger parish and group ministry plans should be thought of by denominational executives as an integral part of the appointive system. As such the continuity of directors can be effected. The director's role can be a position of status and responsibility for the minister who has a sincere desire to be a town and country pastor and has been trained for the position.

One of the major problems in The Methodist Church has been how to promote a minister who has done acceptable and outstanding work in a rural charge. The traditional pattern has been to advance the pastor to a larger church with more responsibility and a larger salary. This type of advancement often means the only available appointment is an urban church. The pastor with a calling to and training for the town and country ministry must make a decision—will he remain in a rural charge at a smaller salary and less status, or will he accept the urban church? Should he decide to accept the urban church, and he has every right to, he will probably be found to live with a guilt complex, feeling he has given up his first love. The Annual Conference of The Methodist Church should make it possible for a minister of the denomination to find expression for his greatest talent, calling, and training. It is to the advantage of the Kingdom and the work of the church to assist a minister to find his place of most efficient service.

The office of director of a denominational larger parish or group ministry offers the type of position within the conference and appointive system which will make normal advancement in responsibility and salary possible. Several larger parish positions can be developed within the conference or episcopal area, making openings for the consecrated, trained minister in town and country areas.[2]

The director is responsible for calling meetings of the ministers. He is to preside at all ministers' sessions. He is to share the responsibility of presiding at sessions of the entire parish with the chairman of the lay council. The director is responsible for the development of the program considering co-operation with: (1) the district superintendent, and (2) the lay council.

It is not the prerogative of a parish director to deal with any aspects of appointments of pastors. This is the task of the superintendent. The superintendent should discuss appointments with the director but should feel complete freedom in making appointments.

Arrangement of the churches on charges is the task of the district superintendent. It is possible that the superintendent will want the lay council and ministers of the parish to undertake a serious study of charge arrangements. Such a procedure would be wise, since it would be a means of bringing the laymen into the analysis of factors involved in charge arrangements. The lay people are acquainted with neighborhood factors such as frictions between families, social stratification, or economic differentials, which make it possible or impossible for churches to work together. Democratic group decisions will lead to a harmonious support of the charge arrangements.

The district superintendent must maintain a close relationship with the parish or group ministry. The structure can become an instrument of administration, making it possible for the superintendent to meet the pastors and lay people periodically. The superintendent should attend as many parish meetings as possible. He should keep in mind, however that *he is in the meeting as a fellow worker*. The director or the chairman of the parish council should preside at the meetings. The superintendent should feel free at all times to enter into discussion but not dominate discussion. This type of democratic group procedure can mean harmonious co-operation. The director should always allow time in the discussions for the superintendent to present any special items of business concerning the district.

The *Discipline of The Methodist Church*, in paragraph 362, 15, *i*, states as one of the duties of the district superintendent the "formation of group ministries, larger parishes, or parish area plans to expedite the work of the church in larger areas." This places upon the superintendent the responsibility of organizing parishes and group ministries. In the normal district, which is predominately rural, the formation of group ministries or larger parishes can be of assistance to the superintendent in several ways: (1) as subdistrict groups, (2) as opportunities to meet with the ministers in groups with stated frequency, eliminating call meetings and special trips, (3) as opportunities, in some cases, for joint quarterly conferences, and (4) as instruments to facilitate the work of the church in every way.

Ministers in a larger parish or group ministry. The role of a minister in a closely integrated larger parish is that of a member of a staff working with others in a definite role of responsibility. It means sharing leadership with a group and being willing to work under the director. If a director uses good leadership practices, there is no need for one to feel subordinate but to have a sense of accomplishment in his own right as he pools his abilities with the staff for the good of the whole.

Friction between persons of a staff often emerge when there is a lack of clearly defined responsibilities. Within a parish staff, responsibilities of each person should be stated in writing so every person on the staff will know exactly his role.

Within the group ministry each pastor is serving a charge. In the charge the pastor has authority and a sense of leadership which gives him security in his own role. Co-operation in the group ministry is essential. He should feel free to assist in planning the program, making suggestions in group meetings. A group ministry is, as the name implies, a group of ministers and congregations ministering in a given geographic area. The staff of ministers and specialized workers function as the staff of a large church—each with individual responsibilities but together serving the whole. In a group ministry the director should seek to discover the special talents of the staff. Such talents as music, evangelism, drama, pastoral visitation, teaching, an understanding of church architecture, stewardship, youth activities, adult education, and ability to write for publication are all needed. Such talents should be shared with the entire group for the benefit of all. This is one of the advantages of group co-operation.

The specialized worker. The specialized worker in a larger parish is usually: (1) a minister, trained in the field of town and

122

country work, appointed as director; (2) a woman rural worker; or (3) a specialist in one of the fields of evangelism, music, or Christian education.

The specialist, other than the minister-director, usually does not have a pastoral charge. He or she is free to work over the entire area, giving assistance where needed. Such persons sometimes find it difficult to fit into group co-operation, and especially to work under the guidance of a director. Friction can arise quickly if there is a feeling of superiority on the part of the specialist. Staff loyalty must be felt. Security comes from doing a good job in one's own right. Caution should always go before criticism. Censure usually arises from a sense of insecurity and a need for more attention. A job well done brings inner satisfaction and eventually a just amount of reward. Teamwork on the part of all staff members is a must.

The lay council. Essential for the operation of a strong parish is an active and functioning lay council. It is composed of representatives from the several churches making up the group. Its primary purpose is to be initiator and promoter of the total program of the group. In a closely integrated larger parish the lay council is responsible for the selecting and employing of the staff. This is not true in the group ministry. In the case of the latter, the pastors who make up the staff are appointed by the denominational body.

The members of the lay council should take their work seriously. They represent their local church and should at all times be in a position to: (1) take back to the local church the plans of the council and staff, and (2) express personal opinion in group meetings and speak for their church.

The council must be creative in thinking with the other members and the staff in developing a program for the group of churches working co-operatively. Harmony will prevail if each

123

member will do his task with sincerity and to the best of his ability.

The chairman of the council should preside at all council meetings and at joint meetings of the council and staff. He should have a carefully prepared agenda and keep the business session moving orderly and on schedule. At all times the chairman should keep in close touch with the director of the parish so plans will be in complete harmony.

There will be numerous subcommittees within the lay council. Each committee should do its work with earnest devotion. The chairman of the council needs to check on committee action to see if it is fulfilling its assigned duties. Ample time should be allowed in the agenda for committee reports.

The official bodies in local churches. The purpose of the larger parish is to strengthen the work of the church in the entire area. In the present organizational pattern of the visible church, this would mean to strengthen the work of the local church. Thus, in a sense, one of the major tasks of a co-operative group of churches is to assist the local church in doing a better job in its own neighborhood and among its own members. This means there must be an active official body within the church: official board, board of deacons, elders, presbyters, stewards, or whatever name the denomination applies to its elected officials. For the sake of understanding, this body is referred to simply as "the board," meaning any officially delegated body of officers within the local church.

The board must feel the obligation to the total life of the parish or group ministry. If there is a constitution in the parish, it should be carefully reviewed periodically. It should be followed by the board and local church. Should the time arise when a board feels the constitution should be changed, a resolution to that effect should be presented to the parish council.

124

Representatives from the lay council should have ample time to report in board meetings any action which has been taken by the council. Dates for council activities should be cleared, proposed programs presented, reports of parish and council activities made. At times the board will ask for time in the Sunday church school or worship service of the church to present announcements and reports. It is essential that a clear channel of communication be maintained between the lay council, the parish staff, and the local church. The board can be the liaison between these groups.

The denominational executive. Reference has been made to the relationship of the district superintendent of The Methodist Church and the larger parish and group ministry. Other denominations have district, synod, county, or regional representatives. Their work will vary a great deal from purely advisory to administrative. In every case, however, the denominational executive is a valuable person in assisting to establish larger parishes and in keeping them operating. Sometimes an executive is in a position to do basic research so necessary in establishing a parish. He may be in a position to inform congregations of the meaning of a parish and advantages which will come from the organization. It is the denominational representative who, in many cases, can be invited into the meetings to organize a larger parish and to assist in bringing the mind of the group together to perfect the program. He can be the "professional assistance" referred to in Chapter III who assists in the organizational process.

The denominational representative must help to keep the leadership in the parish of top quality. He is responsible for assisting the lay council to find leadership when a change is necessary. He can also function as a liaison between the parish, parish leadership, and the connectional organization of the denomination or denominations involved.

Qualifications of a director of a larger parish or group ministry.
The success or failure of a co-operative program is dependent, to
a large degree, upon the qualifications of the director for his
position. A director's role is not easy. He must have the ability
to lead others without the authority of a superior office. He must
have an understanding of human nature to the degree of ability
to cope with differences of personality characteristics, educational qualifications, theological prejudices and interpretations,
and the psychological make-up of individuals in the staff. Four
main qualifications of the director are presented for consideration on the part of one who is considering being a director, and
to assist those persons who are seeking a director for a parish:
(1) an appreciation of rural life; (2) a consecration to the task
of service in the rural church; (3) a knowledge of rural social
systems and rural sociology; and (4) an understanding of basic
leadership procedures.

1. *An appreciation of rural life.* A director must be in sym-
pathy with rural life, feeling that there is a definite contribution
rural people make to the total culture. One of the basic theories
of sociology is that there is always a tendency for urban culture
to dominate the total thinking of a people and that rural life is
minimized in importance. This is reflected in the fact that there
is always a migration of population from rural to urban areas
except in time of catastrophe, such as war or famine. The bright
lights of the city attract the attention of the nation. There is a
premium placed upon the professional man who makes a success of his work in the city—doctor, lawyer, teacher, minister.
One who does a successful work in a rural area is seldom recognized until he has had the stamp of approval placed upon him
by the city. A parish director must be mindful of these facts.
He must be willing to work in the framework of this knowledge,
accepting the role for the merits in the case. These merits are

126

legion. Someone has said that the rural areas of America are responsible for supplying "beauty, bread, brains, and babies" for the nation. This is true, and the 61,000,000 people making up rural America play a vitally important part in the total culture of the nation. Rural life has within it the basic qualities of community which have the opportunity to emerge naturally. Urban areas are cold and impersonal—individualistic—which leads to selfish, noncommunity spirit. The parish director must feel his task is important in the whole economy of the nation. It is important in his denomination. It is important in the universal church.

If a director feels his task is simply to use the position as a steppingstone to a better position or a more prominent one in his church, he had better refuse the position. He should feel this task is one of the most important positions in the church.

2. *Closely related with the sense of appreciation of rural life is that of a sense of consecration to the task of serving the rural church.* With a shortage of qualified ministerial leadership in most of the leading denominations of the nation and the glamour of a rapidly growing urban culture with all the opportunities for establishment of new churches, it is easy for one to lose his sense of mission to rural America. The Protestant churches do not recognize the rural pastorate in equal proportion to the urban, or even with equal proportion to the missionary who serves in a faraway land. There has grown up a feeling that the minister who remains in a rural pastorate or leadership in the rural church somehow could not prove himself a capable leader for a larger responsibility. This is a phenomenon with which a parish director must reckon. He must be willing to face this fact, knowing full well certain recognitions will probably never come his way which do come to some ministers in his denomination. A sense of mission, a sense of calling, how-

ever, has always marked the prophet, and he has been willing, without complaint or defensiveness, to continue his work in the light of a task to be done. The director must live in a constant state of consecration—as should all ministers for that matter—holding the basic elements of the gospel ministry uppermost in his mind. It is helpful to keep in one's thinking the statements of Christ: "Even the Son of man came not to be ministered unto, but to minister"; "The servant is not greater than his lord"; "Whosoever will be chief among you, let him be your servant."

3. *A knowledge of rural sociology and rural social systems* is important to the parish director. There was a time when it was felt a rural minister should be well versed in agriculture so that he could, to a certain degree, serve as an agricultural consultant. In a day of specialization, when there are from one to ten full-time employed agricultural specialists in most counties in America and when theological training is a long and tedious process, the minister does not have time to train in agriculture, nor is there the need for it. He should, however, have enough training in modern agricultural methods to appreciate them and to guide the farmer within his parish to the specialist within his county. He should know how to work with the agricultural extension agent, the vocational agricultural teacher, the soil conservationist. He should be acquainted with the services available from the agricultural college within the state. His parish should be a means of contact for various social and agricultural agencies. This means the director must know the people who are working in his county. He must have a close working relationship with them. He should be a member of farmers' organizations in the area, provided he can agree with their policies. They can be of assistance to his people, and he can be of assistance to them.

The director should have enough work in rural sociology and rural church administration to understand something of the nature of rural society. This will facilitate his getting along with people and his appreciation of the unseen forces which play in the minds of rural people. Group solidarity, intimacy of kin, clannishness, slowness in acceptance of new ideas, a reverence of tradition, all are marks of rural culture. The parish leader will recognize these and adjust his work to fit them rather than oppose them. If a director has not had the opportunity to study rural sociology formally, he should arrange for short courses or additional seminary work, or courses in a department of sociology in a college or university. Constant reading in the field assists in keeping one abreast of scholarly developments.

4. *An understanding of leadership procedures.* The field of leadership as a study is comparatively new. Literature is being produced by sociologists, business and church administrators, and psychologists which make available many books and periodicals in the field.

The director must be able to get along with people. In the church there are few situations where a minister is in authority over another minister. In the episcopal form of government, certain officials—district superintendent and bishop—are delegated such authoritative positions, but a minister, though he may be a parish director, is still a minister among many. For this reason, the parish director must understand fully democratic leadership methods. He must be capable of throwing himself fully into the democratic process of group procedure, realizing that true democracy in group action is the most permanent form of group control. He must be winsome in personality, sincere in his motives, and have the ability to share with the ministers in the parish successes and failures. Precept and example is the best rule to follow. A task well done in his own responsibilities will speak loudly to the other ministers in the staff. A fellowship of the ministers which emerges through informal group gatherings, frequent family dinners, occasional parties and picnics, will go a long way in breaking down any barriers between the members of the staff.

One of the problems faced in a parish staff is the diversity in training by the ministers. Because of a shortage of ministers in many denominations, hundreds of men and women are being used as pastors who have not had the advantage of formal education for the ministry. There is a tendency on the part of the untrained to hold rather dogmatic ideas on theological beliefs which are defended with great emotion, and to feel that the trained person has "lost his passion" for the gospel. This makes for a decided barrier between the director and some members of the staff. Such barriers can be overcome with profound appreciation on the part of the director for the untrained minister who, in his own right, has a genuine call to the Christian ministry and a sincere desire to serve the church. Humility on the part of the director, appreciation for others, and a recognition of the contribution every person on the staff can make to the thinking of the group will aid in overcoming barriers of difference in education. Too much cannot be said regarding the necessity of a director to be brotherly, sincere, and honest in every respect in his working with the members of the staff.

SOME SUGGESTIONS FOR LEADERSHIP

The director of a larger parish or group ministry is in a strategic position to take advantage of good leadership techniques. Only a summary statement is made here, and it is hoped a director will study the books listed in the bibliography.

The democratic process. A parish director should use the process of group discussion with a full understanding of its values, and a sincere desire to find the will of the group. By obtaining opinions, ideas and points of view of fellow ministers and laymen, a strong support will be secured. People will support ideas they have shared in formulating. By sincerely seeking the opinion of others, a creative thought process takes place. By pooling thought, much more can be accomplished than one person expressing his ideas alone.

With group thought permitted and sought, there is a tendency to unearth the dissatisfied person. He has a chance to "get it off his chest." Perhaps his gripe is justified. It should have expression. If it is not justified, expression serves as catharsis helping him to rid himself of his peeves.

Certainly no leader is indispensable. The parish will continue after he is gone. The democratic process of recruiting a large number of people for leadership makes for a permanent program. The more persons who assist in formulating ideas, the larger will be the support.

Democratic action is slow. It calls for patience. Often a director will become weary in waiting for a consensus and support of an idea. But wait he must if he is to succed in his democratic action.

It goes without saying that a parish director must be able to make decisions and sometimes is forced to act upon his own judgment, but every effort should be made to sense the opinions of others. The parish director must: (1) have some goals thought out in his own mind that are flexible in their final conclusions; (2) be completely open-minded to suggestions and ideas of others; and (3) be willing to change his mind and plans as he sees the will of the group with whom he is working. Leadership is like harmony in music, it is something of a gift. One must develop his sense of understanding of others if he is to lead a group. When there are hidden animosities or a lack of support of some move to be taken, it is better to seek harmony. It will pay.

The staff meetings. The director is a presiding officer in staff meetings. He should see that the place of meeting is congenial and comfortable. Many staff meetings have been hampered by the director standing in front of the first pew of a church sanctuary with the members of the staff seated as if in church. Get the members, including the director, around a table—all seated. Make the meetings completely informal. Parliamentary rules should be taken for granted but not rigidly enforced. Group agreement on various items is better than a formal vote.

Respect the opinions of others. Members of a staff, regardless of educational qualifications, have good ideas and contributions to make. Listen to the ideas. They may be immature, but they may contain seed-thoughts which can develop into dynamic action.

Tact. Probably the most needed quality for a director is just plain tact. The dictionary defines tact as: "A quick or intuitive apprehension of what is fit, proper, or right; fine or ready mental discernment shown in saying or doing the proper thing, or especially in avoiding what would offend or disturb; skill or facility in dealing with men or emergencies." Tact can be expressed in the following ways:

1. Honor and reverence members of the staff as fellow Christians and fellow ministers of the gospel.

2. Share all honors which come to the parish. Success will come in a larger parish or group ministry. The director is the one on whom honors will be bestowed. He will do everything in his power to share the honors with the total staff.

3. Express gratitude. A phone call, a note in the mail, an appreciation dinner, will go a long way in assisting to keep harmony in the parish. Such expressions should be to laymen as

132

well as fellow staff members. A district superintendent wrote a note of thanks to a hostess for her courtesy shown him as a guest in her home. She wrote to the superintendent stating that in fifty years she had entertained at her table fifty-two ministers, and he was the first to say "thanks" through a letter. Jesus had something to say about the nine lepers who failed to come back after their cleansing!

4. Sincerity, integrity, and consecration on the part of the parish director will instill confidence from his fellow workers.

5. Be cautious about abruptly going against traditions of the community. Customs in rural areas are deep. They may be meaningless to an outsider, or even offensive. If such customs need to be changed, they can be changed with time and tact. On his first Sunday in a new charge a pastor criticized the children's choir, which had just sung a song he felt was not of worshipful quality. Needless to say the choir died a natural death immediately, and it took more than a year to revive it.

Good sense, good judgment, patience, and above all, a sincere love will reap great rewards for the Kingdom.

An ancient proverb is well worth heeding: "A friend is not made by giving advice—but a friend is made by seeking advice."

RESEARCH IN PREPARATION
FOR A LARGER PARISH
OR GROUP MINISTRY

The establishment of a co-operative program should be preceded by sound research and survey. One of the pitfalls of larger parishes and group ministries has been the failure of leaders to recognize the natural forces of population, social groups, topography of the land, and economic factors, as they establish parishes. Brunner, for instance, in his 1934 study of the larger parish, realized parishes must have two physical factors to survive: (1) they must be a natural sociological unit, that is, rural community; and (2) they must have sufficient economic resources to support themselves in normal times. To these criteria could be added other factors such as a sufficiently large number of Protestant prospects to make the churches adequate to support a program, a spirit of co-operation between congregations and ministers, a willingness of the people to pool financial and leadership resources, the unreserved support of the central town church, and a population which shows signs of enough stability for continued progress.

Not infrequently church leaders have plunged into a parish organization without sufficient knowledge of the ecological factors of the life of the population, only to find an organizationally impossible situation facing the parish. Time, energy, and disappointment will be saved when one does comprehensive research in preparation for the parish. Research findings when presented in graphic and tabular form will assist the people of a local area to understand more fully their need for a co-operative undertaking by the churches.

The research does not need to be exhaustive; nor does it need to be done by a specialist. If special help is available from a denominational executive, professor of sociology, or a professor of church administration, such help should be used. It is possible, in some situations, that a study be done by a student or a group of students as a project in a college or seminary course.

The basic items for research are presented in this chapter. A detailed questionnaire to be used by the local congregations is presented in Appendix B. Additional helps are suggested in the bibliography.

DELINEATION OF NEIGHBORHOOD AND COMMUNITY

The basic essential of a closely integrated larger parish, interdenominational or denominational, is to confine the parish to one rural community. A loosely integrated larger parish or group ministry can function efficiently if it embraces two or more rural communities provided they are a part of an enlarged community. The definitions of these meaningful sociological units are reviewed to freshen them in the mind of the reader.

"A rural community consists of the social interaction of people and their institutions in the local area in which they live on dispersed farmsteads and in a hamlet or village which forms the center of their common interests." "An enlarged community is two or more rural communities bound together in a natural or political area with a dominant town in which all communities find a common interest." A review of Chapter I will assist in understanding these basic structural units of rural society.

In establishing a closely integrated larger parish the delineation of the rural community is necessary, and the boundaries of the parish should not go beyond the community. People will work together intimately in a rural community. They are accustomed to face-to-face relationships in school, church, trade, and social activities. They will not work closely together beyond community lines. Within a closely integrated larger parish there is one budget for several churches, and two or more employed workers serving the entire parish. The parish council must serve as one board directing the work of the parish. The churches must have affinities sufficiently strong to override suspicion and friction.

In the loosely integrated larger parish or group ministry, each minister serves one or more congregations and derives his support from his charge. The parish council is not concerned with dispensing salaries to ministers. It assists the work of the local church but is not an "official board" in the administrative sense that it is for the closely integrated parish. Therefore, the loosely integrated parish or group ministry can cover more than one rural community. When it does, it should not go beyond one enlarged rural community. In the enlarged rural community there is one dominant town such as the county-seat or leading trade center, and two or more subdominant towns. A subdominant town is smaller in population and is able to offer fewer services than the dominant town. There are enough ties between the people of an enlarged rural community to warrant a loosely organized co-operative parish as they look to the dominant town for agricultural specialists, hospital service, and other professional leadership.

To delineate means to define. It can be recalled that one of the characteristics of the rural community is that it can be defined. It has geographic limitations. Among rural sociologists the delineation of the rural community has been done most effectively by determining common areas of trade and other areas of social interaction.

It was near the beginning of the century that a young sociologist accidentally discovered a method of delineating the rural trade community. Charles J. Galpin reported in 1911 on his work in Walworth County, Wisconsin:

Take the village as the community center; start out from here on any road into the open country; you come to a home, and the deep wear of the wheels out of the yard toward the village indicates that this home naturally goes to this village for trade, doctor, post office, church, lodge, entertainment, high school; the next home the same, and the next and the next, until by and by you come to a home where the ruts run the other way and grass grows a little perhaps in the turn toward this village, and you find that this home goes to an adjoining town for its major associations; between these two homes is the bounding line of the community.[1]

Thus the trade area of a central town becomes the community area according to Galpin's discovery. This discovery has been explored by many researchers since that date, and the methods of community delineation have been based upon the assumption that where people derive their primary (that is, oft repeated) services, such as groceries, school, church, doctor, entertainment, they will develop a community solidarity.

137

There are two primary ways of determining the trade or service area of a rural community. The first method is the modern sequel to Galpin's observations. Most states now place on county maps the average traffic flow per twenty-four hours at stated points along highways and secondary roads. The traffic-flow meter which operates by photoelectric cell, or with a rubber

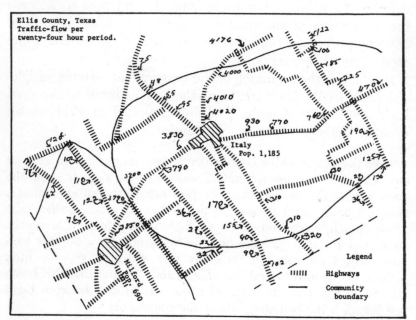

Source: Traffic-flow map of Ellis County, Texas, Texas Highway Department, Texas Highway Planning Survey, Austin.

FIGURE X. Ellis County, Texas, traffic flow per twenty-four hour period. By finding on each highway and secondary road the point of lowest traffic flow per twenty-four hour period, it can be assumed that that point is the dividing line between communities. Connecting the points of lowest traffic flow around the town will determine the trade-area community.

138

tube across the highway, is a common sight to the motorist. For a nominal sum, usually not more than one dollar, a traffic-flow map for a county can be obtained from the state highway department. By finding on a given road the low point of traffic flow, it can be assumed this is the point of division between two trade centers to which local residents go for their primary services.

Circumscribing a town one can find the low figure of traffic flow on each road. Connect these points by a line, and the trade area community is defined. Figure X illustrates the process showing a section of the traffic-flow map of Ellis County, Texas. The communities and neighborhoods in Figure I were delineated by the traffic-flow process.

The second method of community delineation is to reverse the process of the traffic-flow method; that is, by starting in the trade center village and working out to the extremity of the community. Page 24 lists the six services needed by all people for normal existence; namely, economic, educational, religious, social, communicational, and professional. By talking with the persons in the trade center town one can secure information as to how far people come for the services. Take a map of the county to the grocer and ask him to spot on the map the homes in each direction whose residents trade at his store. Do the same for the garage operator, the service station operator, the banker, the doctor, the local newspaper editor. Ask the high school superintendent to plot on the map the homes at the extremity of the service area of the school. Connect the homes for the different services, drawing a line around the village or town. The areas for each service will not be the same, but it will make a fairly well-defined configuration revealing the trade-area community.

It will be discovered that the larger the town, the larger will be the community. In a simple general science experiment there

139

is a demonstration of the power of a magnet. With a magnet beneath a sheet of paper, iron filings are dropped on the paper. Immediately the magnetic force is seen in the configuration of the iron filings around the magnetic poles. This is an elementary illustration of the "pull" of a trade center in a community. Naturally the more services a trade center can offer and the farther it is between trade-center towns, the larger will be the community. It is a safe hypothesis that a closely integrated larger parish will operate within a community delineated in the above fashion. It is possible that racial, ethnic, or class factors will enter in which will make for a lack of harmony. These factors do not appear in delineating the community by the trade-center area.

The enlarged rural community consists of one dominant town and two or more subdominant towns with their surrounding rural neighborhoods. The enlarged community is delineated in a similar manner to the rural community. The county is used as a basis for beginning the study. Many counties across the nation are becoming "communitylike" since the central town, usually the county seat, supplies all of the services needed by the individual. In such a town will be a small hospital (one or more), several lawyers, a public park, a library, and dealers in farm machinery, automobiles, and large appliances. Professional help such as an agricultural extension agent, a soil conservationist, and a home demonstration agent are in the larger town. Many central towns have the office of the regional Farm Bureau, Grange, or Farmers' Union.

A good place to start in delineating an enlarged rural community is to take a map to the county agricultural extension agent. He will be able to point out the affinities of persons within the county, and their dependence upon the central town. He can point out natural barriers such as unbridged rivers,

140

mountains, lakes or forests which keep people from making the central town their trade center for buying large items, such as farm machinery and automobiles.

Should there be two dominant towns in a county, it is quite likely there will be two enlarged communities. Figure I, mapping Ellis County, Texas, shows clearly two enlarged communities in the county with the central towns of Waxahachie and Ennis respectively.

It is possible that the enlarged community might reach beyond the county line. A rural neighborhood across the county line can be dependent upon one of the subdominant towns for primary trade and associations. The political boundary is not as strong as trade ties.

With the development of the consolidated school, it has been discovered that rural community boundaries, and the extent of influence of the enlarged community, are being redrawn to conform to the consolidated school boundaries. Ties made by children and young people in their associations in school activities are very strong.

The final test of a rural community and enlarged rural community delineation is by actually asking a series of questions of residents near the edge of what the researcher thinks, based upon his preliminary study, is the boundary of the community. Sometimes, to save travel time, the questionnaire is put into the hands of children and young people in school. This method is not as reliable as the actual house-to-house visit but will be sufficient to begin the work of a parish. Questions such as the following should be asked:

1. Where does the family buy groceries?
2. Where does the family go to movies?
3. Where does the family buy gasoline?

4. In case a piece of farm machinery is broken during harvest, where does one go to buy small repair parts?

5. Where does the family buy cars?

6. Where does the family go for a medical doctor?

7. Where does the family go if in need of hospitalization?

8. Where does the family go to church?

9. Where do the young people attend high school?

10. Where do the children go to elementary school?

11. Where does the family attend Farm Bureau, Grange, or Farmers' Union meetings?

12. Where does the mother in the home buy the winter wardrobe for herself and family?

Space can be left at the end of each sentence to write in the name of towns. It is possible to put the names of town into the questionnaire and simply ask the persons to check under each item.

Questions 1, 2, 3, 4, 6, 8, 10 and 11 are indicative of rural community relationships. These are primary services, or oft-repeated services, and are usually available at the rural community trade-center. Questions 5, 7, 9, and 12 are guides to the enlarged rural community. With the exception of attendance at high school, they are services which are not needed often. Consolidation of schools in many cases has made the dominant town in an enlarged community more important.

A little practice and careful observation in community delineation will aid the novice in rural sociology to become efficient in understanding the natural groupings of the area under study.[2]

POPULATION ANALYSIS

Population is people, and people are the mission of the church. Therefore, what is happening to population is of vital importance to the church.

In an area being considered for a larger parish, a thorough analysis of population should be made. The published reports of the United States census of population are the best information. Reports are available in public libraries, college libraries, or can be bought for a particular state for a nominal sum.[3]

If a more detailed report of population for a segment of a county is desired, it can be secured through a special order from the Director, Bureau of Census, Washington 25, D. C. Unpublished data for a township, for instance, can be supplied on census enumeration areas along with a map showing the areas. Such information will cost approximately fifteen dollars per township.[4]

The trend in population for thirty to fifty years should be traced. The smallest population unit should be used, e.g., town, township, or population precinct. Figure XI shows Nevada County, Arkansas, a typical rural county, with township divisions. Table I is typical of how trends can be reported. In this manner a very small segment of the county can be examined. By placing the churches on the map (as is done in Figure XI for one denomination) the trends in the area of the church can be studied. A comparison of trends in church membership over a stated period of time, and in population over the same period of time can reveal if the church is keeping pace or losing ground.

The internal composition of population should be examined. Helpful data to be compiled are: (1) white and nonwhite, (2) urban and rural farm, rural nonfarm, (3) age-sex distribution, (4) employment status, and (5) educational achievement. All of these items can be secured from published census reports. The use of the material is dependent upon the ingenuity of the leaders of the parish.

All materials should be graphed and charted. This provides

NEVADA COUNTY, ARKANSAS

Table 1. Population Changes by Minor Civil Divisions, 1900 to 1950

NO. TOWNSHIP, TOWN OR CITY	1900	1910	1920	1930	1940	1950	CHANGE 1900-50	%CHANGE 1900-50	CHANGE 1940-50	%CHANGE 1940-50
TOTAL	16,609	19,344	21,934	20,407	19,869	14,781	−1,828	−11.0	−5,088	−25.6
1 Alabama tp	1,004	1,139	1,116	1,125	948	687	−317	−31.6	−261	−27.5
2 Albany tp	1,462	1,464	2,194	1,752	1,467	925	−537	−36.7	−542	−36.9
3 Boughton tp	1,199	1,337	1,224	1,046	903	678	−521	−43.4	−225	−24.9
4 Caney tp	962	1,100	1,277	1,145	1,390	931	+ 31	− 3.2	−459	−33.0
5 Emmet tp	653	867	1,182	1,007	1,020	782	+ 129	+19.7	−238	−23.3
Emmet t	277	270	420	387	465	482	+ 205.	+74.0	+ 17	+ 3.6
6 Georgia tp	580	833	785	675	651	408	− 172	−29.6	−243	−37.3
7 Jackson tp	1,011	1,061	1,173	867	644	379	− 632	−62.5	−265	−41.1
8 Leake tp	880	730	742	897	834	554	− 326	−37.0	−280	−33.5
9 Missouri tp	3,956	4,978	5,635	5,814	6,188	5,741	+1,785	+45.1	−447	− 7.2
Prescott c	2,005	2,705	2,691	3,033	3,177	3,960	+1,955	+97.5	+783	+24.6
10 Parker tp	1,423	1,629	1,900	1,615	1,484	888	− 535	−37.6	−596	−40.2
11 Redland tp	1,028	1,389	1,545	1,126	1,129	775	− 253	−24.6	−354	−31.3
12 Taylor tp	1,344	1,531	1,934	2,188	2,211	1,423	+ 79	+ 5.9	−788	−35.6
13 Union tp	1,107	1,286	1,227	1,150	1,000	610	− 497	−44.9	−390	−39.0

Estimated population, 1956: 12,902. There are 1,246 Methodists in the County, or 17% of white population.

Negro population: 5,315.
Median school years completed: 8.2.
Source: U. S. Census of Population: 1900 to 1950.
A Survey of Methodism in the Little Rock Conference, 1956, by Marvin T. Judy.

a visual way of presenting the data to individuals and groups.

ECONOMIC ANALYSIS

A stable population and a stable church are dependent upon a stable economy. Information should be secured for the area under study which will give some basis of judgment as to the stability of the area. Sources for the study are published reports such as the Farm Census (available through the United States Department of Agriculture), business reports of the chamber of commerce, farm bureau, state universities, and utility companies. Many states have organizations composed of numerous agencies who pool their resources to promote economic enterprises. Such organizations will make available their published information.

Nevada County, Arkansas, is again used to illustrate. For the years 1949, 1952, and 1953, the estimated total income for Nevada County was, in millions of dollars, 8.6, 9.4, and 9.6 respectively. The estimated per capita retail sales in 1953 were $429, and the estimated per capita income for the same year was $749. The last two figures in comparison with the state average are $919 and $1,017 respectively. It will be seen that Nevada County is below the state average.

Additional information for Nevada County is supplied in Table 2.

Table 2. Selected Statistics for Nevada County, Arkansas, from Farm Census of Arkansas, 1954 and Prior Years.

YEAR	NUMBER OF FARMS	AVERAGE SIZE OF FARMS (ACRES)	AVERAGE PRICE PER ACRE	IRRIGATED FARM LANDS (ACRES)	ELECTRICITY	TRACTORS	CATTLE	HOGS	CHICKENS
1954	1,420	135	44.00	65	1,251	421	17,746	3,215	42,247
1950	1,827	113	34.00	5	1,254	322	12,324	4,007	46,338
1945	1,995	105	23.00	—	301	94	11,896	4,299	65,263

Source: Selected statistics from the Farm Census of Arkansas, 1954 and Prior Years. Prepared and published as a service to members by the Arkansas Economic Council.

To assist further in understanding the economic condition of a region, the level of living for farm families can be secured.[5]

The level of living index is based on 100 as the average for the nation. Therefore, below 100 or above 100 indicates the status of the county in comparison with the national average. The index is usually based upon four items: (1) per cent of farms with electricity; (2) per cent of farms with telephones; (3) per cent of farms with automobiles; and (4) average value of products sold or traded in the year preceding the census (adjusted for changes in purchasing power of the farmer's dollar).

Nevada County, Arkansas, has the following level of living indexes for the years 1930, 1940, 1945, 1950, and 1954: 34, 30, 37, 64, and 86 respectively. It will be observed that the county falls below the national average. When the farm statistics for 1955 are observed, however, there is a clear indication that through irrigation and a changing from raising chickens to cattle, the income is rising. Value of land has increased and the size of the farm has increased. Though population is decreasing in Nevada County, Arkansas, there is a better economic base for those who are remaining.

PARISH RESPONSIBILITY AREAS

The Protestant Church has never taken seriously the geographic parish as has the Roman Catholic Church. Among Catholics definite boundaries are drawn for a local congregation. When a family moves into the parish, the church membership is automatically moved to that parish. Protestants have left the choice to the individual as to which congregation he will join, and to which congregation he will transfer his membership.

Protestants should, however, have "parish responsibility areas." That is, lines should be drawn between congregations designating the area for which the local church is responsible for pastoral care and evangelism. Such parish boundaries do not confine the initiative of the individual, but simply designate responsibility

146

areas. In this manner no person is left without the responsibility of a church. Many studies have revealed large sections of population outside the responsibility areas of existing congregations.

The first step in establishing responsibility areas is to discover the territory the churches are actually serving. This is done by asking the ministers to plot on a map the homes in which there are members of the local congregation. When the memberships are put together on a master map, a configuration of parish areas will take shape. Lines reaching the members on the extremity of the parish can be drawn around each church.

A more simple, though not as accurate, method of determining parish areas is to prepare a sheet containing concentric circles. In the center is located the church. In each direction from the church the pastor will draw in roads. He will place a dot on each road locating the home of the farthest resident-member from the church. These dots are connected with an irregular line around the church. The area enclosed is the territory the church is actually serving. By placing on a master map the parish area, overlapping responsibility territory can be discovered, and areas unreached by any church will be revealed. Figure XI has the parish areas of the Methodist churches of Nevada County, Arkansas.

THE HOUSE-TO-HOUSE CANVASS

To secure accurate information on church potentials, nothing will exceed the house-to-house canvass to secure data from which the religious nature of a community can be discovered. To make a house-to-house canvass over an extensive territory, however, is a very large task involving a great deal of time. If the larger parish or group ministry has a full-time employed staff member serving the whole area, the house-to-house canvass can be a project of that person. It is not wise to undertake a study on a wide scale

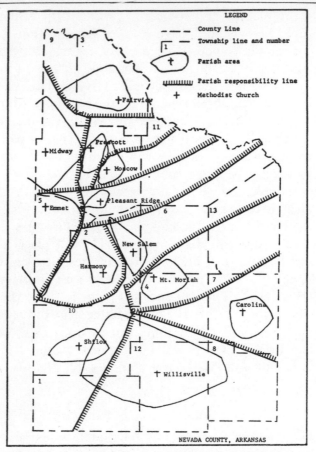

Source: *A Survey of Methodism in the Little Rock Conference,*
1956, by Marvin T. Judy.

FIGURE XI. Nevada County, Arkansas. The above map is illustrative
of four major areas of research in preparation for a larger parish or
group ministry: (1) location of all churches in the denomination
involved, (2) location of the parish area of each church, (3) parish
responsibility lines, and (4) township lines and township numbers.
Table 1 shows the population trend by townships.

with voluntary help until a larger parish is well under way. Sometimes in the enthusiasm of a newly organized parish, someone will suggest as the first joint project of the parish a census of the whole area. This sounds good, but when faced with the reality of making such a census, the spirit of the parish is frequently hampered. The matter of a parish-wide house-to-house canvass should be postponed until the parish is well organized and there is an adequate staff to give leadership to such an undertaking. Generally a parish is not ready for this type of work until it has been organized for at least two years.

When parish responsibility lines have been plotted on a map for each local church, there will usually be some part of the larger parish or group ministry which is not being reached by any of the existing congregations. If this is the case, such as is found in townships 6, 11, and 13 of Nevada County, Arkansas, in Figure XI, a concentrated study can be made of such a section by all churches of the parish. A house-to-house survey should be made to determine how much church potential there is and why the residents of the area are not being reached by the existing congregations. Such a study may reveal the need for organizing another congregation. It might reveal a heavy ethnic group who are members of another congregation not co-operating in the larger parish. It might reveal a large percentage of Negro population.

DATA ON CHURCH ORGANIZATION

To secure a broad understanding of the church in its existing state, data should be secured concerning the ministry, church building, parsonage or manse, historical information, organizational structure, church school, and other timely information. To secure such information a questionnaire can be placed in the hands of each minister. He should be instructed to secure the

149

assistance of a lay committee to answer all questions. When information from each church is compiled by a central committee, or by one individual, the total church situation in a given area under study can be secured.

To assist in research on the local church a detailed questionnaire is given in Appendix B.

Epilogue

This book should not be brought to an abrupt close with the emphasis on research. There is far more to a larger parish than sociological forces, maps, graphs, and statistics. There is more to a larger parish or group ministry than careful, well-planned meetings. There is more to a co-operative program than good leadership requirements.

The larger parish or group ministry is a philosophy. It will work only as long as the leaders possess the spirit of service—service to all persons within the parish by all ministers and congregations. The spirit of Christ must permeate the entire procedure, or techniques and methods simply become tools inadequate to do a task so desperately needed in the rural United States.

Love must be the dominant motive of all leaders. A love akin to the New Testament *agape*. A love which loves when there is little response. A love which loves when there is even hostility. A love which loves when there are few material rewards. But a love which will eventually find response, bringing revival to old churches and strengthening the work of the Kingdom.

Far back in the mountains of eastern France will be found two rural churches—Waldersbach and Fouday. These churches were served by John Frederic Oberlin who lived from 1740 to 1826. Oberlin, a Ph.D. from the University of Strasbourg, gave himself without reservation to his mountain parish for fifty-nine years. He has become the patron saint of the rural ministry.

Near the end of his life he wrote a prayer for his parish which was read at his funeral. Within the prayer are the elements of love of a pastor for his people, a shepherd for his flock. May this love permeate the leaders, pastors, and congregations in Rural America!

Thou, O ever dear Parish, God will not forget you, nor abandon you. He has thoughts of peace and mercy for you. Oh! that you might forget my name to remember only that of Jesus Christ whom I have preached. He it is who is your pastor. Good-bye, dear friends, I have loved you much. O my God, may thine eye ever watch over my dear parishioners, thine ear be ever open to hear them, and thy hand be ever stretched out to protect them. I commend them to thee, and put them in thy arms. Send them pastors after thine own heart and never leave them.[1]

Appendix A

From the thirty-five Larger Parishes studied by Ralph A. Felton, a constitution was written which includes the main items needed to carry on such an organization.* It is given here with the hope that it may be useful to groups of churches, pastors, or denominational leaders wishing to organize a Larger Parish.

THE CONSTITUTION OF THE LARGER PARISH

ARTICLE I. NAME. The name of this organization shall be the _____
Name
Larger Parish.

ARTICLE II. PURPOSE. The purpose of this Larger Parish is to minister to all the people within its area by a program of activities that can best be carried on by the co-operation of several churches.

ARTICLE III. MEMBERSHIP.

Section 1. Any church within the area may become a member of the Larger Parish when it desires by showing a willingness to do its part in all the undertakings of the parish and upon adoption of the constitution and election of representatives to the council.

Section 2. Any church may withdraw from the parish if the council has been given notice of said intention three months beforehand.

Section 3. All persons who are members of the co-operating churches also become members of the Larger Parish.

ARTICLE IV. THE LARGER PARISH COUNCIL.

Section 1. The Larger Parish Council shall be the governing body of the Larger Parish.

Section 2. The council shall be composed of four representatives from each church: the Sunday-school superintendent, a young person to represent the youth, a member of the governing body of the church,

* Ralph A. Felton, *The Art of Church Cooperation*, Dept. of Town and Country Work, The Methodist Church, New York, 1948. Used by permission.

and a woman to represent the women's organizations. Any other person who is a member of one of the churches may attend the meetings.

Section 3. The officers of the council shall be president, vice-president, secretary, and treasurer.

Section 4. The council shall meet every three months. One of these meetings each year shall be for the election of officers and the consideration of finances.

Section 5. All members of the staff shall be ex-officio members of the council and may attend all meetings and may be elected to office.

Section 6. The council shall plan the program and activities for the parish.

ARTICLE V. THE STAFF.

Section 1. The staff shall be composed of the pastors of each of the co-operating churches, the denominational supervisors of each, the directors of religious education, the music director, and the summer workers.

Section 2. There shall be a chairman and secretary elected by the staff. The chairman shall preside or appoint someone to preside at all staff meetings. The secretary shall keep a record of all meetings.

Section 3. It shall be the work of the staff to co-operate with the council in carrying out the activities and program decided upon by the council. Each member of the staff may be assigned to various committees to help guide the activities.

ARTICLE VI. FINANCE

Section 1. Each church shall continue its local and denominational obligations as before it became a member of the Larger Parish.

Section 2. Each church is responsible to the Larger Parish only for amounts that have been pledged by the church. But each church shall be expected to share its part of the financial affairs of the parish.

Section 3. All money for the Larger Parish shall be paid to the treasurer, who shall pay all bills upon the vote of the council.

ARTICLE VII. DENOMINATIONAL RELATIONS.

Section 1. The program of the Larger Parish shall not interfere with the denominational practice or program of any of the co-operating churches.

Section 2. Interdenominational fellowship shall be one of the goals of the Larger Parish.

ARTICLE VIII. RELATION TO OTHER ORGANIZATIONS.

Section 1. The Larger Parish shall co-operate wherever possible with all the organizations that make for community improvement.

Section 2. Special emphasis shall be placed on the importance of co-operation with the schools within the parish.

ARTICLE IX. AMENDMENTS. Amendments to this constitution shall be presented to the staff and then presented to the council. If two-thirds of the members present at the council meeting vote for the amendment it shall become effective immediately.

Appendix B

To assist in research for preparation for a larger parish or group ministry, a questionnaire is given in Appendix B. The questionnaire is one used by the author in a study of the Little Rock Conference of The Methodist Church.*

When questionnaires are used, every effort should be made to secure complete and accurate data from each church involved in the study. A study is good only insofar as the information is complete.

*The questionnaire is adapted from one prepared by Roy A. Sturm, Director of Research and Surveys, The Methodist Church, 1701 Arch Street, Philadelphia 3, Pennsylvania. It is used by permission.

Study Guide

_____ District

_____ Pastor

_____ Address

_____

A. The Church in the Community.

1. Name of church _____ Charge _____.

2. P. O. Address _____ Town _____
   County _____ Township _____.

3. Number of churches on charge _____. (*A study guide should be prepared for each church on the charge.*)

4. The church is located in: open country ___; village or town ___; city ___. Population, if known _____. If a city church, it is: downtown ___; residential ___; suburban ___; other (specify) _____.

5. If church is in town of 2,500 or *less*, or open country, from what distance can the church be reached with good roads? _____.

6. How far is the nearest church of the same denomination? Blocks _____; miles _____.

7. Is the church well marked with a sign or signs? _____. A bulletin board? _____.

8. Does the charge provide a parsonage? Yes ___; No ___. How far from this church? Blocks _____; miles _____.

9. Where is the pastor's study located? Church ___; Parsonage ___; none ___.

10. The minister:
    How many years have you served in the ministry? _____.
    How many years in present charge? _____.
    How many charges have you served? _____.
    Education: Please fill in the following table:

156

	YEAR ATTENDED	NAME OF SCHOOL	YEAR GRADUATED	DIPLOMA OR DEGREE
High School				
College				
Seminary				
Other				

B. *History and Organization.*
   1. In what year was the church organized? _____.
   2. Has the church ever sponsored the formation of another church? Yes __; No __. A church school? Yes __; No __; Dates _____
   _____.
   3. What is the status of the sponsored group at present? Active __; Inactive __; Dissolved __.
   4. This committee believes that a survey to determine the need of a new church should be conducted in the area of _____
   _____.
   The boundaries of this area are:
   a. Northern limits. Street or highway _____.
   b. Eastern limits. Street or highway _____.
   c. Southern limits. Street or highway _____.
   d. Western limits. Street or highway _____.

C. *Building and equipment.*
   1. In what year was the present building erected? _____. Date when last finished (redecorated) inside? _____. Additions were added to building in the years _____.
   2. What is the general condition of the church building(s)? Good __; Fair __; Major repairs needed __. Condemned __.
   3. What is the general condition of the parsonage? Good __; Fair __; Major repairs needed __. List the major repairs needed
   _____
   _____

4. How many rooms in the parsonage? _____. Do they provide adequate living space for the minister's family? Yes __; No __.

5. Does the parsonage have the following equipment: Central heat __; gas heat __; refrigeration __; electricity __; plumbing complete __; plumbing partial __; power washer __; complete furnishings __; air conditioning __.

6. Are the church buildings and equipment considered adequate for the needs of the congregation? Yes __; No __; Explain _____

D. Finances.

1. How much was raised for all purposes last year? _____ (Amount reported in last conference journal or denominational year book.)

2. List the approximate amount of the budget raised last year from the following sources: (consult your church treasurer for accuracy.) Contributions of members through systematic giving $_____. Special offerings (such as Easter, Christmas, etc.) $_____. Endowments $_____.

3. Is the church engaged in a special building fund campaign? Yes __; No __. If yes, give goal for campaign $_____; collected to date $_____; pledged to date above collected $_____.

4. How many members following consistent systematic giving? _____ (pay regularly to church weekly or monthly). How many members of the church tithe? _____.

5. Is there an annual every-member canvass to secure pledges to underwrite the budget? Yes __; No __.

6. Has the church any indebtedness? Yes __; No __; Amount $_____.

7. For what reason was the debt assumed? _____ _____.

8. How long has it been carried? _____. How is it being taken care of? _____.

9. If financial aid is received from outside the church, list where: Conference or association board of missions __; Sustentation or minimum salary fund __; General board of missions __. Amount in current year $_____. How many years has there been such aid? _____.

E. Membership.

1. Number of church members reported in last conference journal or year book _____.

2. Number of church members who do not live in the immediate vicinity of the church. These might be called nonresident members _____.

3. Number of people listed on the constituency roll or prospect roll. _____.

4. What is the average attendance at Sunday morning church worship service for the past six months? _____. Evening service _____.

5. During the past five years, how many young people from this church have entered the ministry or mission field? _____.

F. Program and Organization.

1. Organizations: fill in the following listings:

	NUMBER OF GROUPS	MEMBERSHIP	NUMBER OF MEETINGS PER YEAR
Woman's Organization			
Men's Organization			
Youth Organization			

2. Check if committees are organized and functioning in the following areas:

	Organized	Functioning
Evangelism	Yes __; No __	Yes __; No __
Education	Yes __; No __	Yes __; No __
Missions	Yes __; No __	Yes __; No __
Finance	Yes __; No __	Yes __; No __

3. Does the church practice the rotation system in the official board or other governing body? Yes __; No __.

4. Activities: fill in the following inventory:

159

	YES	NO
*Public worship every Sunday morning		
Public worship every Sunday night		
Services two Sunday mornings per month		
Services one Sunday per month		
Regular midweek service		
Special evangelistic services held last year		
Special Holy Week observance		
Daily vacation church school in last year		
Weekday religious education for children		
Mission study classes held		
Church membership preparation classes		
Envelopes used weekly or monthly for offering		
Regularly adopted church budget		
Permanent membership record		
Alphabetical membership record		
Evangelistic visitation teams		
Lord's Acre program		
Regular choir (4 or more voices)		
Children's choir		
Delegates to youth camp		

	YES	NO
Clinic or dispensary		
Supervised playground or gym		
Monthly family nights		
Weekly church bulletin (enclose a copy)		
Weekly or monthly church paper (enclose copy)		
Regular radio program		
Regular television program		
Regular newspaper space bought		
Sponsor Boy Scouts		
Sponsor Girl Scouts		
Part of group ministry		
Church is member of interdenominational council, either city or county		

*List here the preaching schedule if above does not apply ————

CHECK HYMNBOOK USED:	SUNDAY SCHOOL	CHURCH
Official denominational hymnal		
Other (write in name)		

TO BE PREPARED BY CHURCHES LOCATED IN COMMUNITIES OF 2,500 POPULATION AND LESS, INCLUDING OPEN COUNTRY

G. The Church and Its Surroundings.

1. How many (more or less) businesses are there in your town now

than ten years ago? More _____; Less _____. (Inquire of long-time residents.)

2. What has been the (increase or decrease) in public school enrollment in the past ten years? Increase ____; Decrease ____.

3. Check the following, considering the majority of people in the community:

	TOWN	DISTANCE
Where do they buy groceries?		
Where do they buy cars?		
Where do they bank?		
Where do children attend high school?		
Where do children attend elementary school?		
Where can a doctor be secured?		
Where do they go for hospital service?		

4. Check the following if a community problem:

_____ Commercial recreation
_____ Poverty or unemployment
_____ Poor roads
_____ Juvenile delinquency
_____ Inadequate leadership
_____ Community conflict
_____ Lack opportunities for youth
_____ Lack community pride
_____ Under churched
_____ Over churched
_____ Poor public schools

5. Number of church members with residence in community who commute daily outside of community for employment _____.

6. Is there a general migration of young people out of the community? Yes __; No __. Explain _____ .

7. Is there any type of community co-ordinating organization made up of various religious and secular organizations? Yes __; No __. If yes, does this church belong to it? Yes __; No __.

MAP LOCATING CHURCH, CHURCHES OF OTHER DENOMINATIONS,
ABANDONED CHURCHES, TOWNS

On this page sketch a map of the territory around the church for a
distance of five miles in each direction. The church of this questionnaire
should be located in the center marked CHURCH. Locate the following
items on the sketch map:

1. Major highways or streets. (Name streets and number highways.)
2. Other churches of same denomination in the area. (Name them on
   map.)

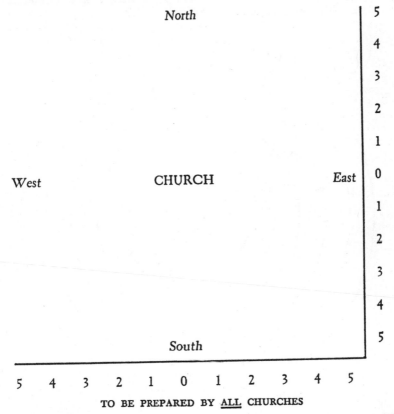

TO BE PREPARED BY <u>ALL</u> CHURCHES

3. Churches of other denominations. (Give denomination and name.)
4. Abandoned churches of same denomination. (Name them.)
5. If a country church, name and locate towns in area.

INSTRUCTIONS:

Each circle represents one-half mile radius from the church.

1. Locate the church at the center of the circle at intersection of North-South and East-West lines.
2. Draw lines representing streets or roads leading from church.
3. Place a dot at the location of each church family living on each road.
4. Connect the dots at farthest extremity, drawing a line around the circles. This is an outline of the parish boundary.

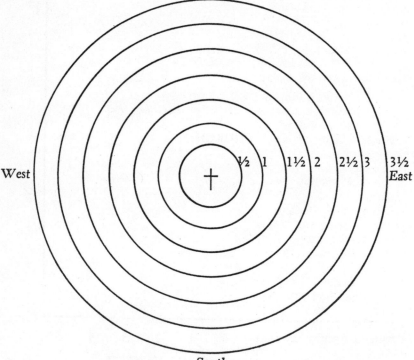

Notes

CHAPTER I

1. For a full discussion see Ch. 4, "Patterns of Land Settlement," Lowry Nelson, *Rural Sociology* (New York: American Book Co., 1955); and Ch. 7, "Settlement Patterns," Loomis and Beegle, *Rural Social Systems* (New York: Prentice-Hall, 1950).

2. Loomis and Beegle, *op. cit.*, p. 187.

3. Lawrence M. Hepple, "Implications of the Missouri Rural Church Study for the Town and Country Church Movement," *New Horizons for Town and Country Churches* (published by the Department of Town and Country Work, National Council of Churches of Christ in the U.S.A., 1956), p. 49. Dr. Hepple's study is reported in Research Bulletins 633A to 633G, College of Agriculture, University of Missouri, Agricultural Experiment Station, Columbia, Missouri.

4. The writer is fully aware of the controversy in recent years expressed through research findings over the validity of the rural neighborhood as an ecologically meaningful social group. There is no question that recent research is proving the tendency of rural areas to minimize the importance of the rural neighborhood in favor of the rural community. This is in keeping with this study, for the trend only heightens the problem of the rural neighborhood church. It must be kept in mind, however, that there are thousands of Protestant rural neighborhood churches still in existence. The work of these churches must be made vital, or the people in the service area of these churches must be reached with a meaningful ministry in new patterns of church administration.

The eight leading texts in Rural Sociology recognize the neighborhood as a meaningful group of associations in rural society. For a further discussion of the subject, see Walter L. Slocum and Herman M. Case, "Are Neighborhoods Meaningful Social Groups Throughout Rural America?" *Rural Sociology*, XVIII, No. 1 (March, 1953), 52-59. See also Alvin L. Bertrand, "Rural Locality Groups: Changing Patterns, Changing Factors and Implications," *Rural Sociology*, XIX, No. 2 (June, 1954), 174. For further reading, see Charles E. Lively and Cecil L.

Gregory, "The Rural Sociocultural Area as a Field for Research," *Rural Sociology*, XIX, No. 1 (March, 1954), 2.

The liveliness of the issue can be illustrated by the fact that in spite of Slocum and Case making a strong and justifiable stand for the deterioration of the rural neighborhood, David E. Lindstrom in *Rural Sociology* XIX, No. 2 (June, 1954) reports research on "Rural Neighborhoods in Illinois," p. 188. In this article, Lindstrom states the use of the rural neighborhood as the basis of research in relationship to re-forming school districts. His article ends: "Without question, the country school district had an important part to play in the formation of the neighborhoods in the country. The new forces of tax differentials, ease of travel, and the attraction of the larger community centers have doubtless had their effects on the natural neighborhoods. But the fact that they could be delineated, even in such counties as McHenry, indicates that they exist—though they may be dormant. It is apparent that their delineation can be useful in determining new areas of social administration or functioning, such as the formation of rural community schools." See J. H. Kolb, *Neighborhood-Family Relations in Rural Society* (Wisconsin Agr. Exp. Sta. Res. Bull. 201: Madison, Wis., 1957).

5. R. M. MacIver, *Community: A Sociological Study* (New York: The Macmillan Co., 1928), p. 22.

6. Kenyon L. Butterfield, *Mobilizing the Rural Community*, Extension Bulletin No. 23 (Massachusetts Agricultural College, 1918), p. 9.

7. Dwight Sanderson, *Locating the Rural Community*, N. W. State College of Agriculture, Cornell Reading course for the farm, Lesson: 158, 1920, p. 417.

8. Dwight Sanderson, *The Rural Community: The Natural History of a Sociological Group* (Boston: Ginn and Co., 1932), p. 481.

9. J. H. Kolb and Edmund deS. Brunner, *A Study of Rural Society* (Boston: Houghton Mifflin Co., 1952), p. 233.

CHAPTER II

1. The reader is directed for further detail on the subject of rural and urban differences to the following works: Sorokin and Zimmerman, *Principles of Rural-Urban Sociology* (New York: Henry Holt & Co., 1929). Ferdinand Tonnies, *Fundamental Concepts of Sociology, Gemeinschaft und Gesellschaft*, tr. by Charles P. Loomis (New York: American Book Company, 1940). L. H. Bailey, *The Holy Earth* (New York: Charles

Scribner's Sons, 1915). Rockwell Smith, *The Church in Our Town* (Nashville: Abingdon Press, 1955), Ch. 1. Rockwell Smith, *Rural Church Administration* (Nashville: Abingdon Press, 1953), Ch. 1. See also list of books on rural sociology in the bibliography at the end of this book.

2. See Mark Rich, *Rural Prospect* (New York: Friendship Press, 1950), p. 20.

3. Arthur F. Raper, *A Graphic Presentation of Rural Trends* (Washington, D.C.: Extension Service and Bureau of Agricultural Economics, United States Department of Agriculture, 1952), p. 8.

4. *Ibid.*, p. 14.

5. See *Farm-Operator Family Level-of-Living Indexes, for Counties of the United States, 1945, 1950, and 1954,* U.S.D.A. Statistical Bulletin No. 204. Alvin L. Bertrand, *Trends and Patterns in Levels of Living of Farm Families in the U.S.* U.S.D.A. Agr. Inf. Bull. 181; Washington, D.C.: Agricultural Marketing Service, 1958.

CHAPTER III

1. See Edmund deS. Brunner, *The Larger Parish, a Movement or an Enthusiasm?* (New York: George H. Doran Co., 1933). Malcolm Dana, *The Larger Parish Plan* (Congregational Church Extension Board, n.d.). Harlow Mills, *The Making of a Country Parish* (New York: Missionary Education Movement of The United States and Canada, 1914). Mark Rich, *The Larger Parish* (Ithaca, N.Y.: Cornell University Extension Bulletin No. 408, 1939). *The Larger Parish and The Presbyterian Church in the U.S.*, Town and Country Dept., 341-B, Ponce de Leon Ave., N.E., Atlanta, Ga.

2. Mills, *op. cit.*, Ch. 3, pp. 25-35.

3. *Ibid.*, pp. 13, 15, 18, 20.

4. *Ibid.*, p. 13.

5. Brunner, *op. cit.*, p. 3.

6. Dana, *op. cit.*, p. 11.

7. Dana, *op. cit.*

8. Brunner, *op. cit.*

9. Brunner, *op. cit.*, p. 67.

10. *Ibid.*, p. 70.

11. Mark A. Dawber, *Rebuilding Rural America* (New York: Friendship Press, 1937).

12. Mark Rich, *The Larger Parish, an Effective Organization for Rural Churches* (New York: Cornell Extension Bulletin No. 408, 1939).

13. *Op. cit.*, p. 4.

14. From a letter dated January 8, 1958.

15. Aaron H. Rapking, "Pioneering in the Kingdom of God" (unpublished), Ch. 7. Used by permission.

16. *The Group Ministry*, Department of Town and Country Work of The Methodist Church, Glenn F. Sanford, Superintendent, 1701 Arch Street, Philadelphia 3, Pennsylvania.

17. H. S. Randolph and Alice Maloney, *A Manual for Town and Country Churches* (Dept. of the Rural Church of the Board of National Missions, Presbyterian Church, U.S.A., 1950), p. 69.

18. A complete bibliography of references to the larger parish as a unit of church administration is given at the end of this book.

19. Ralph A. Felton, *The Art of Church Cooperation* (Madison, N.J.: Drew Theological Seminary, 1948), p. 33.

20. Calvin Schnucker, *How to Plan the Rural Church Program* (Philadelphia: The Westminster Press, 1954), p. 110.

CHAPTER IV

1. Material supplied through correspondence with Mrs. Anita Guyton, secretary for Macon County Larger Parish, and the annual parish reports.

2. Material supplied through correspondence with the Rev. Frank Turnbull, director of the Dale Hollow Larger Parish, and a paper by Vinton D. Bradshaw. Also *Town and Country Church*, April, 1958.

CHAPTER V

1. One cent rate will be effective until July 1, 1960.

2. See North Central Regional Publication No. 17, *Family Farm-Operating Agreement* and North Central Regional Publication No. 18, *Family Farm-Transfer Agreement*, available from state agricultural colleges extension service. *Establishing Methodist Families in Town and Country*, Department of Town and Country Work, The Methodist Church, 1701 Arch Street, Philadelphia 3, Pennsylvania. Ralph A. Felton, *A New Gospel of the Soil*, Department of Rural Church, Drew Theological Seminary, Madison. N.J.

3. An excellent guide for community analysis can be secured from

Iowa State College, Agricultural Extension Service, Ames, Iowa. Ask for *Guides for Building Your Tomorrow's Community* by W. H. Stacey.

4. Mills, *op. cit.*

CHAPTER VI

1. Brunner, *op. cit.*, p. 55.

2. There has been a debate for many years as to the advisability of a minister taking special training for the rural pastorate. Some church leaders hold that a minister should choose the rural or urban pastorate, or specialized ministry such as chaplaincy, teacher, or counselor, and train for that field, remaining in it all his life. Others hold that training should be general and that the minister should simply fit into the appointive system as normal opportunity for advancement presents itself. The writer finds a third position; namely, all ministers in their training be introduced to the work of the church in all areas: rural, urban, chaplaincy, teaching, counseling. If there is a feeling of a special call to one or the other ministry, elective work should be taken in seminary training in the field of choice. Some ministers who feel special adaptabilities to the rural or urban ministry should do advanced work beyond the B.D. degree in the field. All ministers, however, should have a sincere appreciation for the work of the church whether rural or urban. It is impossible to segment the work of the church. "If the hand says to the foot . . ." The urban pastor must feel a sincere concern for the rural pastor, and vice versa. There is no lesser appointment in the Christian cause. For this reason, there should be no stigma on the minister who spends his life in the rural pastorate. There should be no feelings of guilt when a rural pastor accepts the urban appointment. There should, likewise, be no feeling of demotion when an urban pastor accepts a rural appointment. A church as dynamic and adaptable as The Methodist Church should earnestly seek to assist every minister to find a release of his greatest talent and training in the type of appointment for which he is best suited.

CHAPTER VII

1. C. J. Galpin, First Wisconsin Country Life Conference: The College of Agriculture, 1911, p. 12.

2. An excellent base map for a county can be secured from the state highway department. When ordering, state the county and size. Most

highway departments have "full-size" (one inch to the mile), "half-size" (one-half inch), and "one-quarter size" (one-quarter inch). Such maps list all roads, schools, churches, cemeteries, rivers, business houses or towns, and residences.

3. Order, naming state, U.S. census of population, number of inhabitants, and U.S. census of population, general characteristics. Order from Superintendent of Documents, Washington 25, D.C. Cost for most states will not be more than 85 cents.

4. Write to the Director of Census, Washington 25, D.C., stating exact information desired for the exact area, and a statement will be submitted showing whether such information is available and what the cost will be.

5. *Farm-Operator Family Level-of-Living Indexes for Counties of the United States, 1945, 1950, and 1954.* Statistical Bulletin No. 204, U.S.D.A. Agricultural Marketing Service, Washington 25, D.C.

EPILOGUE

1. Augustus Field Beard, *The Story of John Frederic Oberlin* (Boston: The Pilgrim Press, 1909), p. 148.

Bibliography

CHAPTERS I AND II

Agricultural Outlook Charts, 1957. U.S.D.A. Washington, D.C.
Hoiberg, Otto G. *Exploring the Small Community.* The University of Nebraska Press, 1955.
Kolb, J. H. and Edmund deS. Brunner. *A Study of Rural Society* (Fourth Edition). Boston: Houghton Mifflin Co., 1952.
Lindstrom, David E. *American Rural Life.* New York: Ronald Press, 1948.
Loomis, Charles P. and Beegle, J. Allen. *Rural Social Systems.* New York: Prentice-Hall, Inc., 1950.

170

Morgan, Arthur E. *The Small Community.* New York: Harper & Bros., 1942.
Nelson, Lowry. *Rural Sociology.* New York: American Book Co., 1955.
Sanders, Irwin T. *Making Good Communities Better.* University of Kentucky Press, 1956.
Sanderson, Dwight. *Rural Sociology and Rural Social Organization.* New York: John Wiley & Sons, Inc., 1942.
Sanderson, Dwight and Polson, Robert A. *Rural Community Organization.* New York: John Wiley & Sons, Inc., 1939.
Sorokin, Pitirim and Zimmerman, Carle C. *Principles of Rural-Urban Sociology.* New York: Henry Holt & Co., 1929.
Tonnies, Ferdinand. *Fundamental Concepts of Sociology (Gemeinschaft und Gesellschaft).* Translated by Charles P. Loomis. New York: American Book Co., 1940.

CHAPTERS III, IV, AND V

Brunner, Edmund deS. *The Larger Parish, a Movement or an Enthusiasm?* New York: The Institute of Social and Religious Research, 1934.
Carr, James McLeod. *Bright Future.* The Board of Christian Education, Southern Presbyterian Church in the United States, 1956.
Dana, Malcolm. *The Larger Parish Plan.* The Congregational Church Extension Board.
Dawber, Mark A., *Rebuilding Rural America.* New York: Friendship Press, 1937.
Felton, Ralph A. *The Art of Church Cooperation.* Madison, N.J.: Drew Theological Seminary, 1948.
The Larger Parish and the Presbyterian Church in the United States. Town and Country Dept. of the Division of Home Missions, 341-B Ponce de Leon Ave., N.E., Atlanta, Georgia.
McConnell, C. M. *High Hours of Methodism in Town-Country Communities.* Board of Missions of The Methodist Church, 1956.
Mills, Harlow S. *The Making of a Country Parish.* New York: Missionary Education Movement of the United States and Canada, 1914.
Randolph, H. S. and Maloney, Alice. *A Manual for Town and Country Churches.* New York: Department of the Rural Church of the Board of National Missions, Presbyterian Church, U.S.A., 1950.
Rapking, Aaron. *The Group Ministry.* Philadelphia: Division of Home Missions and Church Extension of The Methodist Church.
Rich, Mark. *The Larger Parish Plan.* Ithaca, New York: Cornell Extension Bulletin No. 408.
————. *The Rural Church Movement.* Columbia, Missouri: Juniper Knoll Press, 1957.
————. *Rural Prospect.* New York: Friendship Press, 1950.
Schnucker, Calvin. *How to Plan the Rural Church Program.* Philadelphia: The Westminster Press, 1954.
Smith, Rockwell C. *The Church in Our Town.* Nashville: Abingdon Press, 1955.
————. *Rural Church Administration.* Nashville: Abingdon Press, 1953.

171

Williamson, Ralph L. *Federated Churches*. Ithaca, New York: Rural Church Institute, Cornell University.

CHAPTER VI

Biddle, William W. *The Cultivation of Community Leaders*. New York: Harper & Bros., 1953.

Blackwood, Andrew W. *Pastoral Leadership*. Nashville: Abingdon-Cokesbury Press, 1949.

Crossland, Weldon F. *Better Leaders for Your Church*. Nashville: Abingdon Press, 1955.

Gouldner, Alvin W. *Studies in Leadership*. New York: Harper & Bros., 1950.

Haiman, Franklin S. *Group Leadership and Democratic Action*. Boston: Houghton Mifflin Co., 1951.

Hepple, Lawrence M. *Group Organization and Leadership in Rural Life*. Columbia, Missouri: Lucas Bros., Publishers, 1956.

Poston, Waverly. *Democracy Is You*. New York: Harper & Bros., 1953.

CHAPTER VII

Smith, Rockwell C. *The Church in Our Town*. Nashville: Abingdon Press, 1955.

Stotts, Herbert E. *The Church Inventory Handbook*. Denver: Wesley Press, 1951.

Young, Pauline V. *Scientific Social Surveys and Research*. New York: Prentice-Hall, Inc., 1956.

Films

None Goes His Way Alone. 16mm sound, black and white or color. A story of the Johnson County, Missouri, Group Ministry.

Working Together. 35mm color filmstrip with sound recording. A description of four group ministries in the United States.

Both films are available at all bookstores of The Methodist Church.

Index

173